Identity, Ethnic Diversity
and Community Cohesion

Identity, Ethnic Diversity and Community Cohesion

edited by
Margaret Wetherell
Michelynn Laflèche
and
Robert Berkeley

Los Angeles • London • New Delhi • Singapore • Washington DC

Editorial arrangement © Margaret
    Wetherell, Michelynn Laflèche and
    Robert Berkeley 2007
Introduction © Margaret Wetherell 2007
Chapter 2 © Henry Tam 2007
Chapter 3 © Nick Johnson 2007
Chapter 4 © Dilwar Hussain 2007
Chapter 5 © Omar Khan 2007
Chapter 6 © Ben Rogaly and Becky
    Taylor 2007

Chapter 7 © Coretta Phillips 2007
Chapter 8 © Simon Clarke, Rosie Gilmour
    and Steve Garner 2007
Chapter 9 © Miles Hewstone, Nicole
    Tausch, Joanne Hughes and Ed
    Cairns 2007
Chapter 10 © Claire Alexander 2007
Chapter 11 © Kate Gavron 2007
Chapter 12 © Bhikhu Parekh 2007
Chapter 13 © Avtar Brah 2007

First published 2007

Reprinted 2009

SAGE Publications Ltd
1 Oliver's Yard
55 City Road
London EC1Y 1SP

SAGE Publications Inc.
2455 Teller Road
Thousand Oaks, California 91320

SAGE Publications India Pvt Ltd
B 1/I 1 Mohan Cooperative Industrial Area
Mathura Road
New Delhi 110 044

SAGE Publications Asia-Pacific Pte Ltd
33 Pekin Street #02-01
Far East Square
Singapore 048763

British Library Cataloguing in Publication data
A catalogue record for this book is available from the British Library

ISBN 978-1-4129-4616-2
ISBN 978-1-4129-4617-9 (pbk)

Library of Congress Control Number: 2006938016

Typeset by C&M Digitals Pvt Ltd. Chennai, India
Printed in Great Britain by
CPI Antony Rowe, Chippenham, Wiltshire
Printed on paper from sustainable resources

FSC
Mixed Sources
Product group from well-managed
forests and other controlled sources

Cert no. SGS-COC-2953
www.fsc.org
© 1996 Forest Stewardship Council

Contents

Acknowledgements

This book is the result of a collaboration between the ESRC Identities and Social Action Programme (www.identities.org.uk) and the Runnymede Trust (www.runnymedetrust.org).

It is our shared belief that policy and academic research are often too far apart. It has been a particular pleasure to work together on this project and at the same time show how policy researchers and academic researchers can learn from each other and work in tandem on areas of common concern and interest.

This book came about as a result of a seminar hosted in September 2005 by the Royal Geographical Society. We would like to thank the RGS for hosting our seminar, and their Head of Education and Outdoor Learning, Steve Brace, for his contribution on the day. His re-interpretation of the RGS archives gave an extra dimension to our awareness of the matter in hand. Kerry Carter from the ESRC Identities and Social Action Programme co-ordinated the seminar and did a superb job deftly coping with competing demands arriving from many directions at once.

We would also like to thank all of those who attended the seminar, giving their thoughts, ideas and reflections on the issues raised and thereby enhancing our understandings.

Moving from seminar to publication has been made much easier thanks to Ros Spry from Runnymede. Ros acted as our project manager and in a wonderfully calm and elegant manner kept the book on track, editing and preparing the final manuscript. We could not have produced the book without her.

Finally, we would like to thank our contributors who have been gracious and generous with their time, and, as you will see from their contributions, insightful and engaging in their writing. They have made editing this collection a pleasure and advanced our understanding of the challenges and complexities we face in studying and understanding our multi-ethnic society.

The Editors
Margaret Wetherell, ESRC
Michelynn Laflèche and Robert Berkeley, Runnymede

The ESRC Identities and Social Action Programme consists of 25 research projects in UK universities focused on identity and social exclusion; identity, community conflict and community cohesion; emerging identity trends and identity and political engagement.

The Runnymede Trust is an independent policy research organization focusing on equality and justice through the promotion of a successful multi-ethnic society. Founded in 1968 as a Charitable Educational Trust, Runnymede has a long track record in policy research, working in close collaboration with eminent thinkers and policymakers in the public, private and voluntary sectors.

Biographical Information on Editors and Contributors

The Editors

Margaret Wetherell is Professor of Social Psychology at the Open University and Director of the ESRC Identities and Social Action Programme. She is a former Editor of the *British Journal of Social Psychology*. She has authored or edited 13 books including *Discourse and Social Psychology*; *Mapping the Language of Racism*; *Identities, Groups and Social Issues*; *Men in Perspective: Practice, Power and Identity* and *Citizens at the Centre*. Her empirical research focuses on race and gender issues and, most recently, citizenship and discursive democracy, while her theoretical work focuses on developing discourse theories and methods for social psychology.

Michelynn Laflèche has been Director of the Runnymede Trust since 2001. As Director, she leads the development and review of the Trust's annual work programme and strategic policy direction. Her own areas of specialization include European policy, employment, citizenship and human rights, youth, and voluntary sector development. She has studied and worked on social justice issues relating to race and gender in Canada, Germany and the UK. Recent publications and presentations include: 'Unlocking the UK's diverse cultural heritage' (conference 2004); and 'Meritocracy and Ethnic Minorities: Face, Race and Place' (*Political Quarterly* 2005).

Robert Berkeley is Deputy Director of Runnymede. A sociologist with a PhD from Trinity College, Oxford, he has led Runnymede's follow-up work to the Parekh Report, with particular emphasis on community cohesion, effective regulation of public services, and involving young people in debates on the future of multi-ethnic Britain. Rob is now responsible for Runnymede's strategic policy research programme, and makes presentations, runs workshops and seminars in the UK and continental Europe, and addresses policy papers to government on issues of current concern. His publications, written mostly for Runnymede's own work programme, include: *Guardians of Race Equality: Perspectives on Inspection and Regulation*

(2003), *Realising the Vision* (2004), *Civil Renewal for All* (2004), *What's New about New Immigrants in Twenty-First Century Britain?* with Omar Khan and Mohan Ambikaipaker (Joseph Rowntree Foundation 2005).

The Contributors

Dr Claire Alexander is Senior Lecturer in Sociology at the London School of Economics. Her research interests are in the area of race, ethnicity, masculinity and youth identities, particularly in relation to ethnography. Her main publications include *The Art of Being Black* (OUP 1996) and *The Asian Gang* (Berg 2000). She is co-editor of *Beyond Difference* (*Ethnic and Racial Studies*, July 2002), and *Making Race Matter: Bodies, Space and Identity* (Palgrave 2005) and editor of *Writing Race: Ethnography and Difference* (*Ethnic and Racial Studies*, May 2006).

Avtar Brah is Professor of Sociology at Birkbeck College in the University of London. Her publications include: *Cartographies of Diaspora*, and *Contesting Identities*; and in co-edited volumes: *Hybridity and Its Discontents: Politics, Science, Culture*; *Global Futures: Migration, Environment and Globalisation*; and *Rethinking Identities: Racism, Ethnicity and Culture*.

Ed Cairns is Professor of Psychology in the School of Psychology at the University of Ulster in Coleraine, Northern Ireland. He has spent 30 years studying the psychological aspects of political violence in relation to the conflict in Northern Ireland. During this time he has been a visiting scholar at the Universities of Florida, Cape Town and Melbourne. He is a Fellow of the British Psychological Society, the American Psychological Association and a Past President of the Division of Peace Psychology of the APA. His most recent book, co-edited with M. Roe, is *The Role of Memory in Ethnic Conflict* (Palgrave/Macmillan 2003).

Simon Clarke is Professor of Psycho-Social Studies and Director of The Centre for Psycho-Social Studies at the University of the West of England. Simon is author of *Social Theory, Psychoanalysis and Racism* (2003); *From Enlightenment to Risk: Social Theory and Contemporary Society* (2005) and *Emotion, Politics and Society* (2006, with Hoggett and Thompson). Simon is a member of the Board of Directors of the Association for the Psychoanalysis of Culture and Society and is Editor of the journal *Psychoanalysis, Culture & Society*.

Dr Steve Garner   is at the School of Sociology, University of the West of England, Bristol since 2003. His PhD, on ethnicity, class, and gender in Guyana, was completed in 1999. He has worked outside academia, as a researcher at the Central Statistics Office, Ireland and on EU projects for local government 1999–2001. Now at UWE he is researching whiteness in the European context and the experiences of countries of traditional emigration becoming countries of new immigration. Recent publications include: *Racism in the Irish Experience* (Pluto, 2003), and *Guyana 1838–1985: Critical Perspectives on Ethnicity, Class and Gender* (Ian Randle Press, Jamaica 2005).

Kate Gavron is a trustee and fellow at the Young Foundation and a vice-chair of the Runnymede Trust. She did research in Tower Hamlets with the late Michael Young throughout the 1990s, and her most recent publication, in co-authorship with Geoff Dench and Michael Young, is *The New East End: Kinship, Race and Conflict* (Profile Books 2006).

Rosie Gilmour is at the Centre for Psycho-Social Studies of the University of the West of England, Bristol. She has worked as a teacher and in market research, where she specialized in qualitative research. Her recently completed MA in Social Anthropology from SOAS enlarged on a special interest in the Middle East, the dissertation dealing with the unveiling of Muslim schoolgirls in France. Currently working on the ESRC project entitled *Mobility and Unsettlement: New Identity Construction in Contemporary Britain*, Rosie has been interviewing in both Plymouth and Bristol.

Miles Hewstone is Professor of Social Psychology and Fellow of New College, Oxford, and has previously held chairs in social psychology at the universities of Bristol and Cardiff, UK and Mannheim, Germany. He has researched and published widely in the general field of experimental social psychology. His major topics of research, thus far, have been: attribution theory, social cognition, social influence, stereotyping and intergroup relations, and intergroup conflict. His books include: *The Blackwell Encyclopedia of Social Psychology*, edited with A. S. R. Manstead (Blackwell 1995); and *Stereotypes and Stereotyping*, edited with C. N. Macrae and C. Stangor (Guilford 1996). His work over the last 5–6 years addresses the topic of 'Cross-Community Contact, Sectarian Attitudes and Forgiveness in Northern Ireland', and he has co-authored numerous articles and book chapters on what he calls 'the most pressing problem of British inter-group relations'.

Joanne Hughes is Professor of Applied Policy Studies at the University of Ulster. Her main research interests and areas of expertise are community relations policy, inter-group contact theory and the role of integrated education in divided societies on which she has published widely. Professor Hughes has directed/co-directed research projects that have examined, inter alia, the relationship between cross-community contact and attitudes to ethnic minorities in Northern Ireland; 'single identity' community relations work in Northern Ireland; the use of partnerships in community governance; and peace education efforts in Northern Ireland and Israel. Reflecting the policy orientation of her work, Professor Hughes has been an adviser to OFMDFM and CRC, she has also been

Director of the Community Relations module on the Northern Ireland Social Attitudes Survey.

Dilwar Hussain is Head of Policy Research at the Islamic Foundation, Leicestershire, and was appointed a Commissioner to the Commission for Racial Equality in April 2006. He regularly lectures and trains on his primary research interests of citizenship, Muslim communities in Europe and Britain, and British Muslim identity, and he worked on the 'Preventing Extremism Together' workgroups set up by the Home Office after 7 July 2005. His most recent publications include *Faithful Cities* (May 2006) for the Commission on Urban Life and Faith, and, with Furbey et al., *Faith as Social Capital* (March 2006) for the Joseph Rowntree Foundation.

Nick Johnson is the Director of Policy and Public Sector at the Commission for Racial Equality. In this role he is responsible for strategic development on issues of integration, diversity, identity and public policy. This includes working to ensure that public authorities meet their legislative and policy targets on race issues. Nick is also an adviser to the Institute of Community Cohesion and has worked as a consultant in the public sector, as a political adviser and researcher, and is currently writing a book on the political legacy of Senator Robert F. Kennedy.

Omar Khan is a doctoral candidate in Indian politics at St Antony's College, Oxford. He has recently been in Delhi pursuing his research on the justification of preferential policies in India. Prior to his doctoral studies Omar worked as a researcher at the Runnymede Trust, and since 2001 he has maintained that connection as a consulting policy researcher. He writes articles and reviews for the *Runnymede Quarterly Bulletin*. In 2006 these included: 'The Theory of Events – Tolerance, Secularism and Groups' (March); 'Grounding Community Cohesion in Democratic Values' (June), and a Runnymede Perspectives Paper entitled *Why Preferential Policies Can Be Fair – Achieving Equality for Members of Disadvantaged Groups* (September), launched at the CRE in November 2006.

Bhikhu Parekh is a Professor of Political Philosophy at the University of Westminster and a Labour member of the House of Lords. He is a Fellow of the British Academy and President of the Academy of Social Sciences. He has published several widely acclaimed books in Political Philosophy, the latest being *Rethinking Multiculturalism*, published by Harvard University Press and Palgrave in 2000. He was Chair of the Runnymede Commission on the Future of Multi-Ethnic Britain. The report was published in 2000.

Dr Coretta Phillips is at the Social Policy Department of the London School of Economics and the Mannheim Centre for the Study of Criminology and Criminal Justice. Her research interests focus on the relationship between ethnicities, racism, and crime and criminal justice, minority perspectives and issues around community safety policy and practice. Her publications include: *Racism, Crime and Justice*, with Ben Bowling (Pearson Education 2002); 'Facing Inwards and Outwards?: Institutional Racism, Race Equality and the Role of Black and Asian Professional Associations', article in *Criminal Justice* 5(4): 357–77 (2005); 'Ethnicity, Racism, Crime and Criminal Justice', chapter co-authored with Ben Bowling in *The Oxford Handbook of Criminology*, 4th edn (OUP 2006).

Ben Rogaly is Senior Lecturer in Human Geography at the University of Sussex, where he also convenes an MA programme in Migration Studies. He is currently researching 'white' migration histories in the UK and the employment of migrant workers in British and Indian agriculture. Ben's books include *Poverty, Social Exclusion and Microfinance in Britain* (co-authored with Thomas Fisher and Ed Mayo), and *Labour Mobility and Rural Society* (co-edited with Arjan de Haan).

Henry Tam is Deputy Director, Local Democracy, Department for Communities and Local Government, responsible for developing a cross-government approach to the engagement of citizens in solving public problems. From 2000 to 2002 he was the Home Office's Director for Community Safety and Regeneration in the East of England. Prior to joining the Home Office, he was the Deputy Chief Executive at St Edmundsbury Borough Council where his duties included corporate management and community development. He is a Fellow of the Globus Institute for Globalization and Sustainable Development, University of Tilburg, the Netherlands. His published books include: *Progressive Politics in the Global Age* (2001); *Communitarianism: A New Agenda for Politics and Citizenship* (1998); and *Responsibility and Personal Interactions* (1990).

Nicole Tausch completed her doctorate at Oxford University, where she is currently a post-doc. Her research interests include processes in stereotype change, intergroup contact and intergroup conflict.

Becky Taylor is a social historian and research fellow based at the Centre for Migration, University of Sussex. Her research interests revolve around the relationship between the state and minority and marginal groups, particularly in the context of the development of the welfare state. These themes are explored in her next book, *A Minority and the State: Travellers in Britain in the Twentieth Century* (MUP, forthcoming).

1

Introduction

Community Cohesion and Identity Dynamics:
Dilemmas and Challenges

Margaret Wetherell
ESRC Identities and Social Action Programme

This book reports from various front-lines of the 'cohesive community', from those engaged in developing, implementing and evaluating community cohesion policies, those researching communities and identities, and from those living in communities targeted by cohesion interventions. The concept of community cohesion has been one of the UK Labour government's most durable frameworks for thinking through issues of ethnic diversity and conflict. It is increasingly proposed as a remedy also for declining levels of political participation and civic involvement. Yet at the heart of the idea of community cohesion remain some profound puzzles about the dynamics of group identities, the tensions between common values and respect for ethnic differences and confusion over what exactly needs to cohere and what a cohesive community might achieve.

The starting point for this book and for our exploration of these questions was a roundtable held at the Royal Geographical Society in the autumn of 2005 organized by the ESRC Programme on Identities and Social Action and the Runnymede Trust. This roundtable brought together academics, policymakers and community workers to debate the connections between identity, ethnic diversity and community cohesion, in the wake of a turbulent summer dominated by the suicide bombings on London tube trains and the Iraq war. We were meeting in a climate where calls from some commentators that the UK should follow France's more assimilationist path had given way to Anglo *schadenfreude* and bemusement as the situation in France then itself deteriorated into prolonged riots and civil unrest. Early public responses to the bombings had opened out into major re-examinations of the principles of multiculturalism, leading many politicians to revive older, more assimilationist, readings of integration. And there was renewed interest, too, in British national identity as a potential super-glue for diverse and divided communities. These embryonic policy themes intensified in 2006 and form the basis for current debate.

Our aim in this book is to try and understand what is at stake in these discussions and consider the ramifications. The first part of the book presents position statements on community cohesion from four different policy standpoints. We hear from Henry Tam, Deputy Director, Local Democracy (Community Empowerment) at the Department for Communities and Local Government. Tam presents his own personal views but his account is informed by his experiences of the challenges facing governments. We hear, too, from Nick Johnson, Policy and Public Sector Director for the Commission for Racial Equality. The CRE took a controversial line in response to the events of 2005 arguing that the UK was sleep-walking into a North American-style ghetto society. Johnson contextualizes this concern and outlines the CRE viewpoint. Part One includes also a statement from Dilwar Hussain, Head of Policy Research at the Islamic Foundation. Hussain describes the development of local community cohesion initiatives for Muslim communities and he reflects on the broad project of community cohesion from the standpoint of a group at the heart of the current policy maelstrom. Finally, Omar Khan outlines the position of the Runnymede Trust, a charity campaigning against social injustice and racial discrimination and committed to building bridges across communities. Khan's concern is with race equality and how community cohesion and associated identity dynamics can be mobilized to that end. These position statements come then from different sources with different interests but sum up some of the main nodes in contemporary policy thinking.

Part Two of the book then turns to the latest social science research on identity and communities. This part presents, in effect, four case-studies. Each case-study is a detailed empirical examination of one context in which issues of community cohesion and identity are particularly salient. Our aim here is not to paint a representative picture of communities in the UK but through detailed work on four contexts to indicate the knot of practical issues around identity and community cohesion which needs to be addressed. This research, funded by the ESRC Identities and Social Action Programme, includes Ben Rogaly and Becky Taylor's work on a group of estates in Norwich and an exploration by Coretta Phillips of ethnic relations in prisons. Miles Hewstone and colleagues report from their research in Northern Ireland examining identity, cohesion and neighbourhood segregation. While in the final chapter in Part Two, Simon Clarke, Rosie Gilmour and Steve Garner report some of the findings from a large qualitative study in the South West of England with white middle-class and working-class respondents.

Part Three of the book then focuses on new directions and challenges. For the authors in this section, the preceding chapters form the springboard from which their reflections and responses can give rise to some new thinking about the way ahead. Claire Alexander picks up the tension between equality and diversity, for instance, and develops a critical and sceptical view of community cohesion as yet another in a long series of strategies attempting to manage and contain diversity. Kate Gavron, drawing on her work with white working-class communities, evaluates the challenge of social inclusion. Bhikhu Parekh, Chair of the Runnymede Commission on the Future of Multi-Ethnic Britain (among his many roles) argues for more clarity around what is meant by multiculturalism and explores contemporary possibilities for identity and identification. Finally, Avtar Brah, a leading scholar in research on identity, considers what kinds of understandings and definitions of identity need to inform future work. How do we need to think about identity – about similarity and difference – to make progress in this area?

The rest of this introduction gives some background, first, on the history of community cohesion and the policy debates and, then, on the identity dynamics implicated. My aim is to summarize the 'argumentative field' evoked by community cohesion, ethnic diversity and identity and give a stronger flavour of the contribution of each of the chapters in this collection.

Community Cohesion: Concept and Policy

A cohesive community is one where:

- there is a common vision and a sense of belonging for all communities;
- the diversity of people's different backgrounds and circumstances is appreciated and positively valued;
- those from different backgrounds have similar life opportunities; and
- strong and positive relationships are being developed between people from different backgrounds and circumstances in the work-place, in schools and within neighbourhoods.
  (Local Government Association, 2006, 'Leading Cohesive Communities', p. 5)

The concept of community cohesion first gained a high profile in the Cantle and Denham reports responding to the 2001 disturbances in UK towns (see Home Office, 2001). These reports argued that some communities in the UK consisted of ethnic groups effectively leading 'parallel lives'. They concluded that this segregation was damaging and needed to be tackled by policies guided by an alternative, positive and indeed utopian notion of the cohesive community. The statement above (taken from current guidance to local authorities) indicates something of what was meant by this alternative. Since publication of the report of the Commission on the Future of Multi-Ethnic Britain – the Parekh Report (CFMEB, 2000) – a cohesive community is defined as having a common vision and shared sense of belonging. It is based on the positive acceptance of diversity and on equality of opportunity. A cohesive community is one where there is extensive contact between groups and large amounts of what sociologists, following Robert Putnam (2000), have called 'bridging social capital' or forms of association that connect across groups rather than forms of association that strengthen ties within groups.

In the wake of the Cantle and Denham reports, community cohesion was taken up as a guiding framework by David Blunkett as Home Secretary, within the Home Office, and by the Office of the Deputy Prime Minister. It was developed in association with several, differently inflected, but closely allied notions such as 'neighbourhood renewal', 'civil renewal', 'social exclusion' and 'sustainable communities'. Community cohesion policies became embedded as the practical theory for community workers and community development activities, and they were translated into community plans implemented by Local Strategic Partnerships. In 2006, this agenda was taken over by the newly created Department of Communities and Local Government and Ruth Kelly is the Secretary of State currently responsible for implementing policy. The government recently set up a Commission for Integration and Cohesion chaired by Darra Singh; as we write, we are awaiting this Commission's report. For a number of years now the concept of community cohesion has been a central plank in policy and it looks set to continue to dominate the political environment.

The principle of community cohesion can be seen as part of a more capacious political philosophy with older communitarian roots characteristic of the current UK Labour government. This broader philosophy seeks to revalue and remobilize civil society (McLaren, 2005). Community cohesion offers, like any policy framework, a particular diagnosis and interpretation of UK society. This is a reading, as we saw, which finds civic alienation, decreasing social interaction and a distintegrating social 'glue' and suggests as a solution the rebuilding of solidarity, the re-vitalizing of communities and measures to break down separateness. On a practical level, as Alison Gilchrist has explained, it is about community workers 'finding ways to mediate conflict, to reduce prejudice and to eliminate discrimination of all kinds' (2004: 10). Cohesion, she says, is about recognizing people's attachments, the ways in which people create 'comfort zones' but also dispelling myths about other groups outside those comfort zones. It is about fostering those casual exchanges, pleasantries and gossip at the school-gates, in shops and pubs and the regular contacts which reinforce what for many people are the 'weak ties' of community based on neighbourhood and place. For Gilchrist, 'cohesion is not about the absence of conflict, but rather a collective ability to manage the shifting array of tensions and disagreements between diverse communities' (2004: 6).

While the desired outcomes might be relatively tangible at the local community level (even if the means for achieving these are not so obvious), at the national level the task is much more challenging. Community cohesion has been interpreted as the need to find unifying common ground which will inspire assent across the board. It rests, as we have seen, on the idea of commonality in diversity – common principles which are shared and enacted by all sections of the community. But it is not at all clear what those common principles might be. The commonality which is emphasized might be simply the rule of the law. Commonality might be simply a shared attachment to a locality or a sense of neighbourhood and place. Alternatively, it could be an agreement to deliberate together democratically whenever a conflict of interest arises or a disagreement about future directions. Common principles could involve a particular definition of citizenship and the rights and responsibilities of citizens; they could invoke a specified set of ethical and cultural values conveyed in a shared code of 'civility' and 'decency'. This code might entail, for example, Muslim women not wearing veils to aid social interaction with others. Or, commonality could imply psychological bonds and shared emotions such as patriotism, using British national identity as the adhesive which holds diverse groups together. Commonality, in other words, could either be about form (the ways in which people should meet together) or content (the substance of a shared identity). As Omar Khan points out in his chapter, community cohesion has been interpreted quite differently by different commentators and any policy document tends to contain layers of these sometimes competing understandings.

In line with the range of ways in which commonality could be understood, community cohesion advocacy runs the gamut from 'hard' options to 'softer' ones. This flexibility is, of course, a useful political resource. Community cohesion could be interpreted as a robust call for an assimilationist version of integration based around publicly enforced allegiance to British values, fearing and rejecting the supposed disruptive power of multiculturalism. 'Hard' versions of this kind tend to heighten the emphasis on commonality and weaken the stress on diversity. Claire Alexander in her chapter in Part Three of this book argues that over time government policy and public debate have increasingly moved in this direction. 'Softer' versions of community cohesion move in the opposite direction – combining the search for overarching commonalities with more emphasis on removing material and economic inequalities, on anti-racist strategies and on the celebration of diversity.

This debate is played out in this book. Nick Johnson, in a manner reminiscent of 'harder' readings of community cohesion, places a great deal of stress on what the CRE perceives as the problem of ethnic segregation. His position statement in Part One pushes the agenda, in other words, further towards commonality and away from diversity. Omar Khan, in contrast, dismisses such trenchant 'parallel lives' analyses of British communities. He rejects what could be called the 'many individuals, many identities but one national community' argument and maintains a commitment to multiculturalism. Bhikhu Parekh in Part Three returns to this issue arguing that what is required is a dialogical, pluralist and interactive understanding of multiculturalism rather than the static, isolationist and relativist readings which Parekh sees as inimical to the project of a 'shared life'.

The balancing act, however, is not just about commonality and diversity. It is also about the value placed on social justice and equality. Nick Johnson, for example, combines a focus on commonality with a strong call for equality. While Henry Tam, in his chapter, argues that not any solidarity is automatically good *per se*. What is required in Tam's view is a 'progressive solidarity'. This, he says, is not about simple-minded applications of social capital analyses to encourage more people to volunteer, ceasing to 'bowl alone', in Robert Putnam's (2000) terms. It is not about flag-waving, Tam suggests, but about a deep commitment to social justice and removing destructive inequalities in power and wealth. Khan similarly argues (see also Berkeley, 2005) that while the aims of community cohesion and related policies are laudable, they have to be set against a context of significant disadvantage across all sectors for minority ethnic group members and often their white working-class neighbours.

Interestingly, all of these authors are sceptical about definitions of community cohesion based on 'British values'. Johnson wonders about the extent to which a uniform British national identity could be imposed. Britishness should be, he says, 'just one part of every citizen's range of identities'. He re-reads supposedly core British values in more general terms as the premises underpinning everyday citizenship. Parekh similarly argues that it is no use exhorting people to be British. Like Johnson and Khan, he prefers a focus on the demands of citizenship and equal rights rather than appeals to vague senses of 'Britishness' as a psychological state or enforced cultural identity.

For those in the policy world, then, the idea of community cohesion evokes difficult territory and complex negotiations between commonality, diversity, equality and the nation. But what does 'community' mean for ordinary people? Is community cohesion motivating? In their chapter in Part Two, Simon Clarke, Rosie Gilmour and Steve Garner report on their research in Plymouth and Bristol and describe what community means for white middle-class and working-class British citizens in the South West. Their material suggests that when their sample focus on and talk about the idea of community, they do find it compelling and motivating. Their voices and stories celebrate the idea of community, the importance of its perceived security and social integration and they are nostalgic for lost communities. For them, as for some policymakers, community is a solution and an obvious good. These interviewees echo Henry Tam's analysis of the causes of the decline of community (greater mobility, more commuting and a more consumerist culture). Interestingly, there are hints too that identification with super-ordinate national identities (British and European) may well be of a different psychological order than investment in local communities – neighbourhood communities may not be inevitably reinforced by an increased focus on nationality.

The narratives from the South West set up such a glowing view of community life that one begins to question the extent of social disintegration hypothesized by some politicians and policymakers. Yet, these accounts also provide evidence for the shadow side of community – the negative 'bonding' capital, the possibilities for group persecution of those who don't conform, the local xenophobias, and the racisms community workers struggle to address in everyday community cohesion activities. The participants in Ben Rogaly and Becky Taylor's Norwich study, as described in their chapter, make similar points. Here again is the emotional charge around the idea of community (what Avtar Brah in her chapter in Part Three calls the 'homing desire') and the negative – as one of their participants evocatively expressed it: 'like living among crabs in a bucket'.

Rogaly and Taylor's study also raises questions about precisely when community becomes a powerful motivating part of people's everyday lives. They argue that much of the time people are not 'thinking community' albeit, as Clarke et al.'s work suggests, they can 'talk community' at any time when requested. The 'community' in practice, then, sits at the boundary of fantasy and actuality, idealized life and actual social life. As Clarke et al.'s work shows, it is a very important resource for people to make sense of their situation, an ideal to frame 'state of the nation' conversations, but it can bear a confused and confusing relation to lived experiences. Where is the community, who is it and what does it translate into?

Dilwar Hussain makes this point very strongly in his statement in Part One describing the projects the Islamic Foundation is working on in Leicester. He notes that many in Muslim communities also find the idea of community cohesion inspiring and motivating and are engaged in active effort to bring, for example, members of different faiths into shared dialogue. However, he remains sceptical about the boundaries of community. Muslims in Britain, he points out, form a set of communities rather than a single community. Would it be meaningful to talk of community cohesion projects between these diverse Muslim communities? The community cohesion debate in the newspapers and in many policy circles seems very firmly premised on the concept of Muslim homogeneity – 'they' are the community which needs to be 'cohered' into white British communities.

Clearly policy plays an important role in constructing community. When communities are multiple (and Hussain describes the hybrid identities of many young British Muslims who may identify as strongly with a locality such as Birmingham as with their faith) the project of 'cohesion' becomes extremely complex. The very act of marking out and defining communities and groupings as ripe for 'cohesion' (and the simple pictures of these groups presented in the media) risks creating the very problem community cohesion policies are designed to solve. It forces people, for instance, to think 'community', think difference and, as Hussain notes, pick out from their everyday material existence with its whole gamut of identities, activities and ways of thinking about oneself just some potentially conflictual emphases and bases for action. Kate Gavron in her chapter in Part Three similarly notes that one of the dangers of national policy and a national focus is to solidify identities and intensify perceived competition between groups. She stresses the importance of local agendas and local projects beyond the abstract generalizations which dog many formulations of community cohesion.

Critics of community cohesion policies have picked up a number of other issues. First, they have questioned the tacit assumption that unity is to be desired at all costs and social conflict automatically feared (Sennett, 1998). They call for community conflict to be handled democratically in the public sphere – properly aired, debated and negotiated rather than avoided through moralizing policy and the construction of artificial harmony. Critics have questioned too the interpretation that the social fabric of the UK is disintegrating and now needs cohering. Many contest the demographic research on which pictures of increasing ethnic segregation are based (cf. Dorling, 2005; Simpson, 2004) concluding that, in contrast, the UK is more integrated than other European societies and, where there are sufficient numbers of ethnic minority group members in an area and thus opportunities for contact, there is evidence of extensive positive interaction. Omar Khan in his chapter argues that it is disingenuous to associate residential ethnic segregation with multiculturalism. In many cases residential segregation reflects structural disadvantage and pre-dates multiculturalist policies. Ethnic disadvantages and inequalities are still entrenched, as Coretta Phillips points out in her chapter, despite substantial government intervention, particularly in its second term (see also Phillips, 2005). Indeed, some have questioned whether the emphasis on community cohesion risks redirecting attention away from economic and social class divisions to ethical and cultural vagaries (Levitas, 1998).

Other critics wonder why the negative bonding social capital of privileged, wealthy white groups is rarely seen as the problem or the target of policy. As already noted, it is disadvantaged ethnic minority communities who tend to be pathologized (see Claire Alexander's chapter and Avtar Brah's analysis of how white European identities and strategies tend to be put beyond question as a taken-for-granted standard for judging others). In many parts of the UK, for example, it is white young people who tend to be less tolerant of other groups than young people from black and ethnic minorities. Many ethnic minority communities have been concerned that the striving for shared values is in danger of taking the culture out of any cultural groups who have come late to British citizenship. Claire Alexander in her chapter, points out that a focus on community cohesion not only places greater onus on citizens but also allows governments to escape some of their own responsibilities – for their inactions as well as their actions. It is notable that the idea of 'institutional racism', for instance, has difficulty finding a foothold within the community cohesion framework, meaning that governments and other institutions are less likely to be held accountable for their failures in the areas of discrimination and entrenched disadvantage. Finally, critics have also noted that the contradictions in government policies mean that potentially beneficial community cohesion initiatives on the ground are often undone by other aspects of the government's response to law and order issues, for example, by foreign policies such as the Iraq war, or public sector privatization (McGhee, 2003).

What can be said in summary then? Governments face a very difficult and challenging set of problems around inter-communal violence, racism, home-grown terrorism, inequality and declining participation in public and civic life. The concept of community cohesion is both a diagnosis of this state of affairs and a rather vague and shaky solution in an area where it is unclear just what policy and governments might achieve. The broadness of the concept has some advantages but it increases the puzzles around implementation. It sets a moral compass and ideal (one which is highly attractive to many but not without its critics). It poses immensely difficult issues of balance between commonality and diversity, equality and security. And, in practice, community cohesion appears to address UK citizens unevenly turning Muslim groups, for instance, into problems while (at worst) the intolerance of white citizens can become celebrated as part of national identity.

It is clear, however, that it is difficult to think about community cohesion without also considering questions of identity. Community cohesion policies contain many explicit, and implicit, assumptions about human nature, practices of self/other definition, assumptions about the routes between identities and social actions and about group processes. The very concept of commonality *and* diversity together which is at the heart of community cohesion challenges us, as Avtar Brah notes in her chapter, 'to think about difference in ways in which it becomes the basis of affinity rather than antagonism'. In the next section, I turn to the identity issues at stake in the discussions in this volume.

Identity Dynamics

In his chapter, Parekh offers a useful formulation of what is meant by identity. 'Identity basically refers to how one identifies and defines oneself in relation to others. It is a way of announcing to the world and affirming to oneself who one is and how one positions oneself in the relevant area of life.' The sociologist Zygmunt Bauman (1996) argues that the question of identity comes particularly to the fore whenever people are uncertain about where they belong. Identity, he says, tells us how to go on in each other's presence. People thus have a major interest in placing themselves within the range of possible identity categories and cultural styles of behaviour found in a society. We also are concerned whether other people accept our claims to an identity as right and proper.

Clearly, the dynamics of identity are going to be relevant to community cohesion (going on in each other's presence) in a number of ways. First, as Khan notes in his chapter, identity is often seen as the problem or the illness and community cohesion as the solution or the cure. Community cohesion policy sometimes aims to move people on from what are seen as overly strong identifications with ethnic, religious and other groups which cause tensions, hatred of out-group members, the wrong kinds of solidarities and misplaced sectarian loyalties. In this formulation community cohesion is an answer to 'identity politics' and community cohesion policy works against the grain of established identities.

Yet, to be effective, community cohesion policy has to develop its own identity dynamics. It can't be about creating 'identity free' zones. Rather, community cohesion policies typically ask people to identify with super-ordinate identities such as 'the community in general', 'the whole neighbourhood' or 'the nation'. The concept of community cohesion can thus seem to have an ambivalent and doubled relationship with identity, trying to intensify some forms of identification on the one hand while loosening the power of others. How does this work in practice? Is there a necessary conflict, for instance, between strong identification with ethnic groups and identification with super-ordinate communities? Is a 'both/and' approach possible? How can community cohesion policies foster new senses of identity in practice and what identity factors are associated with positive community relations?

Some models of identity would suggest that community cohesion will always be an impossible project – for cohesion, commonality and solidarity to arise on one level, discord, difference and conflict must exist on another. This model suggests that the 'psycho-logic' of identity works against and will always be toxic for community cohesion. Avtar Brah in her chapter notes that many philosophers of identity, for example, have pointed to the profound dependence of identity on 'otherness'. Logically, we discover who we are by defining who we are not. This seems to suggest that the only way a community divided by ethnicity and other identity groupings can achieve common identification and solidarity is through discovering a common enemy – some third group who can be the 'other' for the whole community. Cohesion interventions, then, risk creating cascades of 'otherness' until – one could speculate – the nation as a whole finally pulls together only as it goes to war with another nation.

Although it is certainly the case that evoking a common threatening enemy is usually an effective way of creating cohesion, none of the authors in this volume would support such a cataclysmic reading of the identity dynamics involved in community cohesion. None suggests that the dynamics of identity and patterns of identification automatically scupper social inclusion or positive cross-group relations. Rather they suggest that identification is multiple, shifting and complex with very little that is inevitable about it. Research on identity and community cohesion suggests a more mundane picture. Various contingent factors increase solidarity, inclusion and positive relations in uneven ways.

In her chapter in Part Three, Avtar Brah argues that identity pulls together conscious, strategic, political and social acts and, more difficult to articulate, unconscious and embedded ways of life.

> Conscious agency and unconscious subjective forces are enmeshed in every-day rituals such as those surrounding eating, shopping, watching football or tennis on television, listening to music, attending political meetings or other social activity. These rituals provide the site on which a sense of belonging, a sense of 'identity', may be forged in the process of articulating its difference from other people's ways of doing things. I have called this desire to belong a 'homing desire'.... (Brah, this volume, pp. 142–3)

As Ben Rogaly and Becky Taylor point out in their chapter, community cohesion policies operate on people's deeply ingrained 'habitus' (to use the sociologist, Pierre Bourdieu's, 1977, term), or taken-for-granted senses of the ways 'people like us do things'. These practices are often a background part of everyday life but may involve moments when 'community' becomes self-conscious. Self-conscious community identities may arise through an act of categorization or intervention from an external agency or through strategic and functional mobilization from inside to achieve a goal such as the building of a community centre, or protest around the closing of a local school. Identities are shifting, multiple and at times deeply saturated with emotion. This is the fugitive, volatile and shifting territory community cohesion policies needs to address.

These accounts note that the multiplicity of identity is likely to be a particularly key factor in understanding community cohesion. People may indeed identify as white English, for example, but they also have many other potential identities based, for instance, on gender, generation, parental status, sexuality, musical tastes, and so on. Alliances of shorter and longer duration can form and dissolve around all the possible bases on which people might be united and divided. Perhaps one aim of community cohesion policy should be to develop the conditions which allow identities and alliances to shift and flow in these ways rather than become stuck on one or two dimensions. In support of this, Hewstone et al. in their chapter note early findings from their ongoing research in Northern Ireland which suggest that the more complex and multiple people's over-all senses of identity then the less likely it is that they will be prejudiced against any particular group. This suggests that a both/and approach is possible. In her chapter in Part Three Kate Gavron points out that for some deprived communities this might mean, paradoxically, strengthening what is called bonding social capital or strong within group ties and senses of identity before interventions to strengthen bridging capital and super-ordinate identities across social groups can be effective. Gavron argues that hopelessness and a feeling of defeat in a group, such as the white working classes in some areas of the UK, create particularly troubled dynamics and that strong and positive group identities can be a precondition for strong and positive whole communities.

It seems clear that the conditions in which groups encounter each other are crucial and different kinds of contact will bring about different solidarities. Here Coretta Phillips's chapter in Part Two is informative. Phillips looks at ethnic relations in prisons, and this proves to be a fascinating case study for understanding community cohesion in the broader UK community. She notes a very interesting finding from recent surveys conducted by NACRO and MORI: that whereas 87% of prisoners held a positive view of relations between ethnic groups, only 59% of the British population held a similarly positive view. This and other work suggests that the very diverse and mixed environments of prisons, surprisingly, lead to more cohesive ethnic relations among prisoners. In part, this effect is likely to be due to the 'common enemy' factor noted earlier. A new super-ordinate identity of prisoner has been created versus the prison officer although the pattern is complicated by different and changing institutional frameworks in prisons. But some of this effect, too, is likely to be the result of increased contact under difficult but shared circumstances – much more intensive contact with members of other ethnic groups than may be occurring outside the prison.

Miles Hewstone and colleagues in their chapter point out that contact between groups with strongly held identities can either lead to increased prejudice and competition due to uncertainty and the anxiety associated with that, or contact can lead to the diametrically opposite result with contact increasing positive attitudes and lessening conflict. The power relationship between groups is clearly important for the outcome. For contact to lead to decreased anxiety and sense of threat groups need to be positioned as equals. There needs to be a cooperative task at stake and common goals in an environment where cooperation rather than competition for scarce resources is encouraged. Contact needs, too, to be legitimated through institutional support. Interestingly, Hewstone et al. argue that although the 'common enemy' approach and the creation of super-ordinate identities does work, these are often unstable solutions to community conflict. They suggest a dual identity model is more effective than the simple re-categorizing of identity (we are all British) and thus they reinforce the view that it is possible to have *both* strong group identities *and* strong whole community identities.

Finally, there is one further aspect to the identity dynamics implicated in community cohesion policies and that is the kind of 'imagined identities' or the identity possibilities and narratives that policy itself sets up and offers to people. I noted in the previous section that community cohesion policy constructs notions of community while in the process of trying to work with communities, and the same is true for identity. But policy is reflexive – it changes the world as it attempts to act on it. The identity narratives that community cohesion and linked policies offer to citizens tend to construct an image of the community-minded, active, engaged, participating, responsible, rather bustling citizen who is both immersed in and beyond culture. As a colleague of mine once commented – 'New Labour likes its citizens to be busy'. We need more empirical work on who is grabbed by these new identity possibilities, in what contexts and with what effects. As McGhee (2003) suggests, community cohesion policies both try to manipulate and re-channel existing identity practices in what are seen as more positive directions and demand a re-education of many people's unarticulated forms of habitus. Yet the point about habitus is that it is in many ways beyond self-conscious and strategic choice, reflecting patterns of socialization with long trajectories, suggesting the difficulties (and presumption) of basing social change on ways of life.

Conclusion

Reflecting on the paradox of unity in difference, Henry Tam has argued (see Tam, 2005) that although unity and diversity look allegedly incompatible they can be made to work together. Tam is concerned with political incompatibilities – liberals are suspicious of unity and conservatives are suspicious of diversity. He concludes:

> But whether diversity is embraced to produce a richer form of community life, or is frowned upon and thus breeds mistrust, is down to a combination of the disposition of those involved and the social policies of their civic leaders. (2005: 29)

This volume, in trying to move this debate along, focuses on and attempts to unpick this question of 'disposition' and analyse current social policies. It explores the new policy agenda emerging around ethnic diversity and ethnic conflict. What emerges is a sense of the complexity of the issue. Recognition of sameness and otherness can provoke all kinds of responses from conflict and xenophobia, to curiosity and interest, to appreciation and desire, claustrophobia and a sense of security in troubled times, and so on. We are beginning to understand better the nature of the contexts of contact and the situations where the discovery of otherness proves troublesome and where it proves constructive – as for example when it promotes a renewed commitment to fairness.

Community cohesion policymakers and community workers are in a situation where a great deal of work is required to translate the big utopian communitarian stories, which guide policy at the national level, into local area policies and then into practices on the ground. These translation processes are uneasy and the paths are uncertain. Much remains uncharted but we know about a number of unpredictable, flexible, sometimes weak, sometimes strong, tools and chains of associations and connections which link identity, community and ethnic diversity contingently together. Our hope is that the collection of research findings, reflections and position statements in this book will help cast more light on the patterns and dilemmas involved and the importance of eschewing the glib in favour of the informed.

PART I

POLICY STANDPOINTS: AGENCIES AND UTTERANCES

Position statements on community cohesion are made from four different policy standpoints.

2

The Case for Progressive Solidarity

Henry Tam
Home Office[1]

For at least the last two decades – since the 'market above all'/'loads of money' outlook of the 1980s provoked a communitarian reaction in the 1990s – critics of social fragmentation have been arguing that we urgently needed to recover a real sense of solidarity. In this article I look at:

- the symptoms of this problem of social fragmentation;
- the merits of different diagnoses put forward; and
- which out of the various prescriptions proposed we should follow.

Symptoms of Distress

What are the signs that people are pulling apart so much so that society may not be able to function cohesively? Many commentators have been struck by the decline in engagement with political processes and institutions. Fewer and fewer people join political parties, and an increasing number are not bothering to vote anymore. In the 2005 general election, there were more people who did not vote than those who voted for the winning party. In case people claim that citizens are now resorting to new means to make their political influence count, it should be pointed out that overall the public does not believe they have much influence at all. The trend has been a downward one. According to the Citizenship Survey, in 2005 the percentage of people in England and Wales who believe they have no influence over decisions affecting their local areas is 61%, the figure for lack of influence over decisions affecting their country is 79%. If people seriously doubt that they can make any difference to public policies, they naturally keep away from what they perceive to be futile political action.

Secondly, there has been concern over the fragmentation of society into what some have described as 'atomistic divisions'. Social capital theorists are particularly preoccupied with the fact that fewer and fewer people are now engaged in group activities outside work. They go off to do their own things individually and even those people who join associations tend to be chequebook members rather than active members. In other words, even when they do join up, they pay their subscription via direct debit but they rarely follow up and do many things with other people belonging to those organizations. What is significant is not so much the overall level of membership, but that membership of single-issue organizations is rising at the expense of membership within organizations that bring people together from more diverse backgrounds to deal with more broadly shared interests. Whether it is race, age or religion-based, there is a growing polarization into sharply defined groups. Instead of people unifying under wider banners, they commit themselves to groups that press for changes on behalf of their exclusive group interests. Instead of people from different backgrounds coming together, for example, to campaign against social injustice, many of them focus on issues that are to be dealt with in relation to a particular race or religion.

And finally, there is the unmistakable rise of consumerist individualism and obsession with personal wealth. One illustrative example is based on the US Monitoring the Future Project (source: Wendy Rahn, University of Minnesota): between 1980 and 1990, the proportion of high school seniors in America who believed that 'having lots of money' was personally important to them rose from 51% to 70%. I suspect the trends are similar in the UK. The role models for young people are all too often pop stars, sporting heroes and film celebrities, and in all these cases, the tendency is for success to be defined in terms of how a few would earn substantially more than the rest. Most probably since the 1990s the percentage of young people who put the pursuit of personal wealth above all else has gone up even further. And it is not just the young. Retail therapy is the mainstream option for people who otherwise feel down or disconnected in modern society.

What these symptoms point to is that the social fabric which holds us together is being corroded. If we do not make democratic decisions together, if we seldom join with others except when it is for a narrow instrumental purpose of getting what we want, and if we spend most of our time thinking about earning money for ourselves to buy enough to validate our self-esteem, then society is at risk of losing its solidarity, incapable of rallying its members to come together for the common good when they will just be inclined to look after their individual selves or groups.

Diagnosis of the Underlying Causes

Having considered some of the symptoms, let us consider how the underlying causes may be diagnosed. It is possible that there are multiple causes at work, and we should avoid the temptation to presume there is some single factor that would account for social fragmentation. Equally we should not hesitate to differentiate between different alleged causal factors when their relative efficacy can be discerned.

Moral Decline

We can start with one that fits a populist mindset, namely, the decline in moral sensibility. Whether it is linked to the decline in religious observation or traditional hierarchies, it is supposed that a shift has taken place, from the deferential and compliant mindset up to the 1950s towards an irreverent and all too permissive moral culture. Given that religions have never ceased to be invoked to justify violence and stir sectarian hatred as much as for the promotion of peace and respect, and traditional hierarchies mask oppression no less than they underpin some degrees of stability, the notion of moral decline has little explanatory force unless it can be unpacked to reveal what has really made people less respectful of the feelings and needs of others.

A Loss of Patriotism

Another favourite diagnosis is to point to a weakening in patriotic pride. In the old days, we are told, people really felt that they were all in it together. But has patriotic pride really declined? In the sense of people being willing to pull together and make sacrifices for the greater good, it is no surprise that under the conditions of the Second World War, for example, with rationing and preparations against an invasion as the backdrop, people were ready to stand together. There is no reason to doubt that were similar challenges to be directed at us today, we would rally together without hesitation. It might be argued that patriotism should be manifested without a national crisis, and that people should feel proud to belong to their country. But in sports or the arts, there is little sign that opportunities for celebrating British successes are neglected. In fact, over the two days of 6 and 7 July 2005, London, fittingly as the capital of this country, demonstrated both patriotic joy in celebrating the announcement of the Olympics coming to these shores in 2012, and national solidarity in standing tall after the 7/7 terror attacks. Patriotism is alive and well.

Social Mobility

Our third contender is the weakening of social ties. On this account, the expansion of social mobility and the disappearance of traditional job security have undermined communal stability. There is no longer a clear-cut 'we' living in long-term communities. More and more, people have to move around – to get jobs, respond to the relentless demands for labour flexibility and deregulation, get closer to 'better' schools to exercise choice – and they never stay put long enough to build up extended families, nurture trust with their neighbours, or join local clubs and associations as part of their general social interactions. With economic forces undermining social stability, we have a clear link to the decline of communal relationships.

Insecure Identities

The fourth proposed factor is related to the third. Economic pressures under a free market culture not only cut down the number and duration of stable community relationships, they also spread a sense of insecurity, even in the face of apparent prosperity. For most of the 20th century, people have anchored their identity to the role they or their spouses have – or had – as stable wage-earners in an established organization, which in turn provided the income and status to define how they and their families fitted into the wider community. However, with the demise of jobs for life, people are told that their employers owe them nothing. They have to develop their own skills and get ready to adapt to changing demands. Loyalty to an employer and dedication are to count for little.

Added to that, with the relentless filtering of workers to select the few for top awards and classify the rest as dispensable, people not surprisingly stop having any sense of long-term allegiance to the companies they work for. People become less inclined to put down work-related social roots, but think more about how they as individuals can cope with the uncertainty of 'portfolio working', jumping from one job to another, with little continuity, but mounting stress and dwindling time for collective activities. Richard Sennett's ideas on respect have thrown particular light on how the displacement of stable organizations by those that reward only the most 'talented' with little regard for others who are left behind, has contributed to the problem of low self-esteem and declining social respect.[2] People who do not feel that they can hold their heads up high, having been deprived of a secure position in society, end up disengaging from and, in the case of their children, disrespecting institutions and social practices.

Power in the Hands of the Few

Last but not least, and certainly connected to the socio-economic diagnosis set out above, is the growth of unfair power distribution. With the post-war consensus to cut down on inequalities pushed aside by the post-1970s obsession with celebrating the success of those who can make the most money, contemporary concern with 'equality' is now firmly directed towards giving people the equal opportunities to outstrip others in wealth and status as far as they are able. People who want to refocus on reducing income and power inequalities are dismissed as backward-looking traditionalists who lack vision. So now not only have a minority of people and the organizations they run amassed a vast concentration of power compared with the rest of society, it is presented as a sign of a dynamic and successful society. Those with less power – and power can only be defined in relation to what others possess – feel more and more alienated, cut out of decisions which affect their lives, marginalized.

This problem is compounded by globalization. Not only at the national level do people feel that there are powerful bodies making the decisions they can never influence, they now face global organizations making decisions that affect their lives. So with a greater concentration of wealth and power in national and global organizations, people's sense of their own civic identity – as citizens who should be equal to other citizens in shaping the decisions and destiny of our shared polity – is undermined.

Prescription for Relief of Symptoms if not Cure

There are plenty of prescriptions on offer. But if we are to direct our attention to those that connect with what appears to be the most convincing diagnosis, then we should concentrate on what builds progressive solidarity. This is to distinguish it from rigid solidarity formed out of imposed compliance to a fixed set of social arrangements wherein people have to fulfil their assigned functions and accept their lot in life. Without entering into a debate about the extent to which this type of rigid solidarity might once have flourished in the UK, it is something few would want to bring about today. People want to be able to improve the conditions under which they, and certainly their children, can live. The challenge is how to open up the channels for individual development while enabling people to retain and cultivate a rich sense of solidarity. It was Durkheim who drew attention to this problem around a century ago in the context of European industrialization, and it remains a critical one today.

In order to build progressive solidarity, it is important to know what may look like attractive components but are ultimately distractions. There are reasons to promote volunteering, faith groups' involvement in charitable work, and corporate philanthropy, but it is vital that we do not mistake their development as in any way key to progressive solidarity. Societies that have higher degrees of progressive solidarity – where people maximize mutual respect through minimizing their power differentials – enjoy healthy community life. But there is no evidence that getting the powerful to donate a negligible portion of their wealth to ameliorate the suffering of the weak, encouraging faith groups to take over the administration of a larger share of public expenditure, or getting the least powerful to do more to help each other cope with life, is going to make those who are excluded from decision-making in society have any greater influence on the key decisions in their society. They may feel more comforted, that they have received more sympathetic support, but at the end of the day, be left as powerless as before.

Similarly, whatever the merits of getting young people to carry out services for free to help their country, or encouraging people to celebrate their nationality (for winning sports tournaments or exercising some of the good characteristics that they uniquely possess in the world), they should not be confounded with having a positive effect on the cultivation of progressive solidarity. Indeed the country which is probably at the leading edge of drumming up volunteering, corporate donations, outsourcing public money to exclusive faith groups, communal celebrations, organizing youth action programmes, and orchestrating patriotic flag-waving ceremonies at every turn – i.e. the United States – is undoubtedly the worst of all developed nations in terms of its deficient progressive solidarity.

I can do no better than recommend Richard Wilkinson's (2005) book, *The Impact of Inequality*, for setting out the varying levels of income inequalities across the world and their implications for a wide range of life chances and social experiences. The evidence he has meticulously brought together makes it clear that if we seriously want to maximize the chance of people having the confidence and abilities to come together with each other and with public institutions in shaping the decisions which affect the destiny of their country, their fellow citizens and their own communities, then we have to redistribute power. One of the most effective techniques used by Professor Wilkinson was to test out the hypothesis that countries and cities with the worst income inequalities would suffer from the worst racial prejudice, violent crime and the shortest life expectancies. According to the evidence set out in his book, this was borne out consistently across the world.

To take just one example, the city with the worst income inequalities in the most unequal country in the developed world – New Orleans. Even without any detailed knowledge of that city, months before Hurricane Katrina struck, one could predict that New Orleans would be one of the least well equipped to cope with any disaster. As the hurricane approached, the rich and powerful left the city rapidly, leaving behind the poor and marginalized who had little influence over securing better support for their plight. The outcome illustrated all too tragically how a city with pitifully little progressive solidarity succumbed in adversity.

The case for progressive solidarity is grounded on our experience of how socio-economic pressures, left unchecked, can weaken communal and democratic bonds so much that citizens are reduced to vulnerable individuals in the face of any challenge that comes their way. People must be empowered both by the government acting to limit and reduce the widening gaps between the powerful and the powerless, and through government–citizen partnerships to enable those with relatively little power to make their influence count.

In practice this means real investment to build up public resources and public institutions to counter the inequalities expanding in the private domain. The myth that people are always better off spending more of their own money rather than having services provided via the state was conjured up to protect the vast advantages the powerful have over others who work longer hours, earn much less, and suffer from shorter life expectancies. It is a myth subscribed to by at least half of the US population. The reason why Western Europeans, especially the Scandinavians, live in societies where citizens collectively are much more ready to support each other for their common good is because they still on the whole see the value of the public realm, particularly in redressing the inequities of the increasingly deregulated global marketplace.

Equally important is a systematic commitment to give citizens the confidence and skills to engage in public policy deliberations, communities the support to organize themselves in reviewing priorities and building consensus, and all public bodies the steer to involve citizens in their decision-making. This underpins the Government's action plan for civil renewal, 'Together We Can'[3] which sets out a strategy backed by 65 action points to wider citizen engagement. These action points commit 12 different Government Departments to contribute to widening the scope for citizens to engage with and influence policies concerning policing, health, the environment, science and technology, schools, support for young people and so on. But the plan itself marks only a starting-point for extending the opportunities for empowerment across all aspects of public life. Its mission is to increase people's power in relation to public policies and develop their sense of efficacy and self-belief in directing the course of their society.

Notes

1 The views expressed in this article are put forward to stimulate discussion and are not to be taken as government policies.
2 Richard Sennett is Professor of Sociology at the LSE and BEMIS Professor of Social Sciences at MIT. Notable among his many publications are *The Fall of Public Man* (1977) and *The Corrosion of Character* (1998).
3 www.togetherwecan.info

3

Building an Integrated Society

Nick Johnson
Commission for Racial Equality

Britain, almost without our noticing it, is becoming a society increasingly divided by race and religion. We are becoming more unequal by ethnicity.

In terms of race relations, Britain is unique in the diversity of racial backgrounds of those who live here and the legislation that is in place to promote race equality. However, like many other countries, Britain struggles to meet the demands of ensuring equality within diversity, and at the same time tackle the challenges posed by the threat of international terrorism, increased immigration, the rise of extremist groups and the changed dynamics of race and culture. For example, consider the increased numbers of those with dual heritage and the influx of white Eastern Europeans. Like many other countries across Europe, Britain too is grappling with the role that faith may play in the public sphere and how that can be managed in a secular society.

Recent disturbances in Birmingham, Paris and Sydney, the London Bombings, the tragic events in New Orleans, and the blurred lines between freedom of speech and incitement to racial hatred succinctly illustrate the challenges faced not only by the Commission for Racial Equality but by all those in the field of equality and race relations, from voluntary work at the grassroots level to the new Commission for Equality and Human Rights.

The London bombings made a big impact on our work. Also, while we should not draw direct comparisons with North America, hurricane Katrina and events across the southern United States have highlighted issues we have probably been ignoring, and how things can go wrong if policymakers do not step in and act before the crisis is upon them.

Community cohesion in some cases has carried the coded message of 'making sure people don't riot', with the success of the policy being judged by the absence of riots and open conflict in the streets. But the corollary of this approach is that by the time the violence erupts, we could find ourselves far beyond the situation we needed to address, with no way back. In the USA, we saw a group of people who socially, economically, culturally and psychologically were all marooned outside the mainstream of society. Where you have a society that is so segregated, equality cannot exist.

This might sound like doom and gloom, but there is complacency in some quarters which we need to address. Do we want to live in a society where 30% of parents in one local authority area in the West Midlands refused to allow their children to go on an educational visit to a mosque because they claimed it was 'run by Al Qaeda'?

For too long policies to deal with the social consequences of migration and diversity have focused more on the 'multi' of multiculturalism and not enough on the common culture (where we talk about cohesion and integration, it is multicultural*ism* as a policy tool that we criticize, not the fact that we are a multicultural society). We have emphasized what divides us over what unites us, and tolerance of diversity has led to the effective isolation of communities. While Britain is a diverse and multi-ethnic nation, multiculturalism as a policy framework is now in danger of emphasizing the divisions within our society and making us more fragmented.

If we ignore these challenges, we give succour to those who argue that our inequality and lack of cohesion is due to our diversity. We must not only argue that diversity does not have to lead to inequality, but go further and argue that true equality in a diverse society depends upon successful integration.

The CRE's Position on Integration

Over the past 18 months, the CRE has been at the forefront of a debate about diversity and identity in Britain today. We have certainly come a long way under Trevor Phillips's leadership in developing and leading on wide-ranging policy discussions.

In debating and discussing ideas around multiculturalism, integration and cohesion, we have explored the ways in which these terms have theories and policies ascribed to them. In many respects, the plethora of terminology is used to describe similar desires in terms of public policy. The wish is to create and sustain a Britain where we can celebrate our diversity, but where difference does not have to mean division, and where everyone has the chance to participate in making the decisions that count.

We believe that the best and most inclusive term for this agenda is 'integration', which we have now made the centrepiece of our work. This is not assimilation, but rather an interdependent combination of factors.

The CRE believes that an integrated society is one where everyone signs up to a single core set of values held in common and defined legally: democracy, equality between men and women, the integrity of the person and freedom of expression. When and where these core values conflict with ancestral cultural values, the core values must always win. It is a society in which the statistical chance of any member of society gaining access to a service, acquiring a job or achieving educational success is reiated not to his or her race, faith, cultural background, gender, sexual orientation or age, but only to his or her talent ambition and desire.

However, we have developed the integration agenda into something more specific. We already know a lot about what an integrated society looks like, and it has three essential features:

Equality: Everyone is treated equally, has a right to fair outcomes, and no-one should expect privileges because of who or what they are.

Participation: All groups in society should expect to share in how we make decisions, but they should also expect to carry the responsibilities of making the society work.

Interaction: No-one should be trapped within their own community, and in the truly integrated society, who people work with, or the friendships they make, should not be constrained by race or ethnicity.

In short, there must be equality for all sections of the community, interaction between all sections of the community and participation by all sections of the community.

Equality

One crucial error we could make is to forget that equality is an absolute precondition for integration. A society in which you can predict the outcomes for any individual by their race or other determining factor is one that is not only unequal but also unable to be fully integrated. From a CRE perspective, we base our concerns on the fact that most ethnic minority Britons are poorer, less well educated, less healthy and less politically engaged than their white counterparts.

In some areas, such as the education of gypsies and travellers, the health of some Muslim groups, and ethnic minority representation on public bodies and local councils, we are moving backwards not forwards. We have legislated against discrimination and yet the differential outcomes between racial groups are stark and pernicious. We have to say that we are still failing when a Black Caribbean male is statistically twice as likely to go to prison than get a university degree, when a Pakistani man will earn on average over £6000 per year less than his white peer with equivalent qualifications and living in the same town, or when unemployment is over one-third higher amongst ethnic minority communities than their white counterparts. In the health service, where over one-quarter of doctors are from an ethnic minority, we see just five or six as heads of health trusts.

While racism exists on its own, it is also inextricably linked with the inequality of ethnic minorities. Evidence of the persistence of racism, as it evolves and adapts to the legal codification of equality principles and consequential behavioural changes in society, can be seen by the disproportionate experience of ethnic minorities in the main public sectors when compared with the experiences of the white majority.

The causes of this inequality have changed over the past 20 years. While the number of reported racial incidents is falling slightly, and a 2005 ICM survey for the CRE has indicated that blatant discrimination or harassment are not found as frequently as in the past, other forms of racism are prevalent. By this, we mean something that could be described as 'stealth racism', which in practice means a series of small, apparently insignificant decisions, incidents or encounters, none of which by themselves could be the subject of court proceedings, but all of which are to the disadvantage of ethnic minority employees or clients. This is also increasingly the case for some faith communities, with religion becoming part of the basis for discrimination and prejudice in ways that it did not do previously.

It must also be borne in mind that it is easier to achieve and measure anti-discrimination than to generate 'deep' or 'thick' equality, where somebody's ethnic background does not affect their life chances. 'Deep' equality goes beyond 'thin' equality, which simply measures equality in terms of position or progress. To achieve this depth, we need equality through the strengthened participation of ethnic minorities in all strands of civil society and enhanced interaction between individuals from different ethnic backgrounds.

Participation

We also know that real commitment to equality in government, in our neighbourhoods and in the workplace will not happen until all communities have a voice. Until all Britons are able to participate in relevant decision-making, services and businesses will never provide for us all equally as citizens and customers.

The CRE is greatly concerned that the number of ethnic minority local councillors fell between 2001 and 2004, that there were fewer ethnic minority people on public bodies in 2003 than in the years beforehand, and ethnic minorities are still grossly under-represented in a number of local institutions such as health boards, school governing bodies and cultural bodies. While we welcomed the election of 15 ethnic minority MPs in 2005, if the House of Commons were to be truly reflective of Britain today, it would have over 60. It is troubling that, in terms of representation, the House of Lords is currently more of an exemplar than the Commons.

Civic participation is much lower amongst certain ethnic groups. If you consistently exclude a group or groups from the processes by which society functions, then they are bound to have fewer positive opportunities and life experiences.

The highest levels of participation can be found in the most prosperous areas, amongst the young and people with free time. The lowest levels of participation are amongst the poorest in society, who are therefore deemed to be partly responsible for the increased levels of inequality, as they cannot expect rights if they do not fulfil their responsibilities. This is not something peculiarly British, as the same can be seen from Robert Putnam's research on the decline of social capital in the United States (Putnam, 2000, 2002). Importantly, he also shows how that decline is not an inevitable, downward spiral – it can be reversed with courageous and ambitious public policies.

Interaction

More and more, communities in Britain live with their own kind. Residential isolation is increasing for many minority groups, especially South Asians. Some minorities are moving into middle-class, less ethnically concentrated areas, but what is left behind is hardening in its separateness. The number of people of Pakistani heritage in what are technically called 'ghetto' communities trebled during 1991–2001, 13% in Leicester live in such communities (the figure was 10.8% in 1991), and 13.3% in Bradford (4.3% in 1991). This is similar to African Americans in Miami and Chicago where the figure is 15% (Mike Poulsen, Macquarie speech to the Royal Geographical Society on 7 September 2005).

We are concerned by the research produced by Professor Simon Burgess and his colleagues at Bristol University, which shows that children are slightly more segregated in the playground than they are in their neighbourhoods (Burgess et al., 2005). Recent research in one London borough's primary schools showed that 17 schools had more than 90% Bangladeshi pupils, while nine others had fewer than 10%. This is a real concern. Not only are the children not interacting with one another, but also the parents will not be. We look to the education system to lead and pave the way to bring people together and bring about change, but the education system is actually going in the wrong direction, with further problems down the line.

Alongside this type of hard, spatial segregation, communities increasingly inhabit separate social, religious and cultural worlds. In 2004, the CRE commissioned research (from YouGov) which showed that most Britons could not name a single good friend from a different race, while fewer than one in ten could name two. When we repeated the exercise one year later, the overall situation had not changed. In 2004, 94% of white Britons had said that all or most of their friends were white; in 2005 this had become 95%, and once again a majority (55%) could not name a single non-white friend. This was true for white Britons of all ages, classes and regions.

However, the 2005 research showed that this separation was increasing amongst ethnic minority communities. In 2004, 31% of ethnic minority Britons said that most or all of their friends were from ethnic minority backgrounds, and this had grown to 37% in 2005. The 47% of ethnic minority Britons who said that most or all of their friends were white in 2004 had shrunk to 37% by 2005. It also remains true that younger Britons are more exclusive than older Britons. It must surely be the most worrying fact of all that younger Britons appear to be integrating less well than their parents.

Many communities, particularly those in a minority such as a racial or faith group, find it increasingly difficult to break out of their isolated clusters, leaving them culturally and sometimes even physically ring-fenced within cities. In these segregated neighbourhoods, ethnic minority communities can feel intimidated and under siege, and neighbouring majority communities can also feel excluded, so the two simply never interact.

Circles of friends are getting more mono-cultural, which is a significant change in the last 12 months. These communities will steadily drift away from the rest of us, evolving their own lifestyles, playing by their own rules and increasingly regarding the codes of behaviour, loyalty and respect that the rest of us take for granted as outdated behaviour that no longer applies to them. This applies just as much to certain white communities, and white ghettos, particularly in rural areas, as it does to some inner-city neighbourhoods.

We need to stress how you can bridge between communities. What are those networks, those spheres and those agencies that bring people together? No-one should be trapped in their own communities, and we want the people you work with, or the friendships you make, to be completely unconstrained by race or ethnicity.

However, a society where most ethnic minority Britons are poorer, less well educated, less healthy and less politically engaged clearly cannot be integrated. It is a big agenda and all three factors are preconditions for an integrated society. Without any one of them, you will not achieve the other two.

Collective and National Identity

Recent political, constitutional and cultural changes have fuelled public discussion about the definition of 'Britishness'. The discussion has encompassed many different sectors, from government to academia to the media, presenting diverse views on British values, institutions and narratives. It is likely to be a battleground in British politics with both Gordon Brown and David Cameron setting great store by making 'Britishness' fit with their own political philosophies.

However, we cannot consider Britishness as and of itself. It is just one facet of the way in which people identify themselves. The principles ascribed to being British are almost entirely consistent with those that people include in notions of citizenship. In seeking to define Britishness, we are also looking for something that can unify people and tie communities together. In that context, we should see it as a manifestation of collective identity and perhaps an overarching bridging tool.

Recent emphasis has been on an emotional identification, a sense of belonging to a broader community, expressed through shared symbols and values. The current interpretation of active participation involves the sharing of risks and responsibilities between citizens and the state. Government looks to expand democratic participation by re-engaging citizens in the decision-making process, particularly in relation to public services.

Any progressive agenda should imply that citizens have a political as well as a consumerist relationship with the state. Among the underlying social values of citizens who are committed to the common good is a collective interest in the aims and objectives of policies which override the self-interest of service users. These values will not be evident in a society where life chances are dependent on individual wealth and ability, so diversity and social capital should be emphasized through positive action and the redistribution of resources.

This is where notions of Britishness, identity and citizenship link explicitly to the integration agenda. The solutions we need in order to achieve full equality, interaction and participation, and the end-result – the integrated society – require a collective and shared notion of what that society looks like, a consensus that it is a good thing, and agreement about how we get there.

The changing nature of British society has transformed social composition and dynamics, brought greater cultural diversity, and altered the sources of power and influence and the distribution of wealth. As a result, many citizens now possess inadequate social rights or lack the necessary resources. Those with the most to gain do not or cannot have a presence in their local community or networks. Deprivation leads to disaffection and social unrest, and the debate on citizenship must address the concerns of the most deprived in the interest of community cohesion. A citizen in a state of permanent dependency cannot be a truly equal member of the community.

The most visible cases of dependency are often migrants. Some current migration policies could therefore be particularly damaging to the forging of any collective identity within Britain. As equality can only exist between economically and politically independent individuals, 'aliens' are undeserving of the honour of citizenship. However, it is in the interest of the host community to bestow the legal and psychological security of citizenship on immigrants to enable them to establish roots, contribute to the local community, invest in social capital and care about integration.

As outlined earlier, Britishness must not be an imposed or dominant identity. It is one part of every citizen's range of identities. As recent CRE research says: 'identity remains a fluid and context-sensitive construct'.[1] Tariq Ramadan (2005) argues that everyone has multiple and moving identities where the context defines which part of your identity is stronger. He uses the example of a vegetarian poet who would pronounce his vegetarianism at a dinner party but would not think it salient at a poetry reading.

Generating and Promoting a Shared Identity

If we are defining Britishness as a positive thing by linking it to citizenship and social solidarity, then we need to know how to encourage it. We need to 'capture a sense of the ways in which identities become more or less salient as a function of the situations in which people find themselves'.[2] This is the so-called 'identity spike'. The decision as to which identities we assert, when we want to assert them and what we want to do with them is ours, but the decision does not take place in a vacuum. While some situations may be of our choosing and a positive thing, be it a social setting or supporting a sports team, others will be a reaction to something. These are likely to be a more defensive assertion of identity. This could be at a personal level when someone is the subject of abuse or discrimination, or on another level in response to the impact of national or international events, such as the war in Iraq, a terrorist attack or hurricane Katrina.

For Britishness to succeed we must seek common, equal citizenship. There must be a general agreement to a set of values based on justice, human rights and social responsibility, and a sense of common belonging so that all groups feel at home. All people must be of equal value and deserve equal respect, and all individuals must have the opportunity to voice their opinion on issues that affect them.

The part of any individual's collective identity that defines them as British is there or has the potential to be there; it is just very low or dormant in many people. We need to look at ways we can cause it to spike, not so that it is dominant or that it replaces another part of that identity, but so that it is strong enough to forge a sense of solidarity, of 'we're all in this together', in society as a whole. If we can equate Britishness and its associated values with collective membership of society, we can promote that. However, it can only be encouraged if we live in a society where there is true equality, interaction and participation.

Implications for Policy

The CRE believes that we need to debate not only these difficult and sensitive issues, but also how to respect the kind of difference that we come across daily. In a sense this would be a general code of behaviour, taking into account cultural, religious and racial differences that would provide a baseline for common agreement on how we conduct ourselves in the public sphere.

For instance, should councils print all their important documents in several languages to encourage participation, or is this encouraging separatism? What should we do about holy days which are not bank holidays? Are judges right to say that school uniform may not be compulsory for the devout, even though for some it is compliant with Islamic modesty?

What this discussion will hope to achieve is to reassert fundamental values. We all obey the same laws, we all respect each other's rights, we all sign up to the equality of women and to equal rights for people whatever their sexual orientation. Also, we accept responsibility for participating in and preserving the integrity of our community and our polity.

This would also serve to provide a starting point that looks at what binds us as communities and an opportunity to negotiate differences without falling into the trap of its being interpreted as 'special treatment'.

Conclusion

The CRE believes we need to focus on this three-pronged integration agenda. The best, fairest societies are ones in which people share experiences and common ambitions whatever their racial, religious or cultural backgrounds. In essence we want to reassert the need for a society based on solidarity, in which everyone's life chances are unaffected by what or where they were born.

This is what we mean when we speak of integration. Not an assimilationist process where some communities are told to leave their identities behind, but a process in which everyone who lives in Britain has the right to every opportunity the country offers and the duty to make every contribution of which they are capable.

To achieve this, we believe that the three legs of the integration agenda go together. Unless we have greater interaction, some communities will find themselves on islands cut off from the mainstream, and suffer the fate of being separate and perpetually unequal. Integration has also to be a two-way street, in which the settled communities accept that new people will bring change with them, and newcomers recognize that they too will have to change if we are to move closer to an integrated society.

Integration is about striking a balance between an 'anything goes' multiculturalism on the one hand, which leads to deeper division and inequality, and an intolerant, repressive uniformity on the other. Any agenda for creating a more integrated Britain should explicitly welcome diversity and reject assimilation. It should also, however, emphasize what unites us as a nation rather than that which divides us.

The challenge of achieving integration is not simply about building bridges across racial or cultural divides. It means coming to terms with racism, and establishing a foundation of shared values and a common citizenship which can successfully be shared by the diverse range of ethnic, cultural and faith communities in Britain.

This is a big agenda. It will not happen without positive action and plenty of effort. The hardest challenge will be to encourage interaction, on top of the already taxing work of fighting inequality and increasing participation. It is here, where policy is least developed and requires most thought, that we can least afford to ignore this challenge.

Notes

1   Research conducted by Ethnos for the CRE, entitled 'Citizenship and Belonging: What is Britishness?' (2005).
2   Ibid.

4

Identity Formation and Change in British Muslim Communities

Dilwar Hussain
The Islamic Foundation, Leicester

Questions of community cohesion, ethnic diversity and identity are intensely debated but often in very abstract ways in political philosophy, in academic colloquia, and in terms of broad national policy frameworks. In this chapter I want to move from the global and the theoretical to the local, describing and reflecting on some projects involving British Muslim communities set up by the Islamic Foundation in Leicester. I will then make some more general points about Muslim identity formation and some of the major factors at work.

The Islamic Foundation was set up in 1973 and currently has about 50 members of staff. I work for the Foundation as a researcher. The main areas of activity for us are in the publication of Islamic literature – we have 350 or so titles on our book list at the moment – and research in three main areas of work: (i) interfaith relations, (ii) economics and (iii) Muslim communities across Western Europe. Over the last three years we've initiated a postgraduate education facility, validated by Loughborough University, for the teaching of Islamic studies. This course currently caters for about 60 MA, PhD and postgraduate certificate students.

Three Projects that Shape a Sense of Identity

Here, I want to discuss three current projects that address the issues of identity, diversity and community cohesion, and then go on to consider some of the dynamics which shape and inform Muslim identities in Britain. We are working in a faith area rather than in race relations, but of course there are many areas of intersection and many similarities. Amid much discussion around communities, community formation and community cohesion, academics now talk of three different types of forces that operate within and between communities: bonding, bridging and linking forces. Two of the projects that I focus on here work on bridging between communities, and one on bonding within.

Values Shared in New Working Relationships

The first is a training course for Muslim Imams and community leaders. It is not an Imam training course in the sense that it's taking young people and graduating Imams, but taking people who are already established Imams who want to work within mainstream areas to provide chaplaincy services – for example to Muslims in hospitals, in higher education, or prisons. We provide a course which over a year upskills and orientates these people. In order to achieve this we have teamed up with the Anglican Diocese of Leicester to organize the course – recognizing that there is extensive experience and expertise in chaplaincy and clergy training in the Christian community. This has been a very positive experience for us. We've learned a lot from the Christian community, and the course itself has been devised with a joint Christian and Muslim group running the course, administering the course, and eventually monitoring and evaluating participants. We rely quite heavily on existing Christian chaplains to provide placements, and as students go through the course there is a requirement to undertake about 40 hours of placement work; work experience that must be done in the actual field of work that the student aspires to go into.

More recently as a development of that relationship, we have signed a memorandum of understanding with a new institution in Leicester, set up by the Christian community there, called St Philip's Centre. We will become a partner in helping Christians to think around their evolving role in parishes and areas where there is a decline in Church attendance and an increasing presence of other faith communities, and how the role and mission of the Church changes and evolves in that particular context.

This project has shown that cohesion activities are especially effective when they bring people from different backgrounds together to work towards a common goal. It is also important to note that this is not a one-way process; we share our understandings about the needs of Muslim communities and learn from the expertise already developed by Anglicans. The outcomes go beyond institutional or policy changes; they create working relationships and spaces to discuss shared values and aims.

Muslim/Jewish Contact – Finding Common Ground

Second, we have worked on a mapping project looking at Jewish/Muslim relationships and contact across the country. This has obviously been quite a controversial area of discussion and debate. The project was led by Alif-Aleph UK (AAUK) and has been supported by the Stone-Ashdown Foundation headed by Richard Stone (Vice Chair of Runnymede and former member of the Stephen Lawrence Inquiry Team), a corchair of AAUK at the time, and we have jointly supervised its research and development. Two researchers have travelled around the country looking at different levels of encounter between Jews and Muslims and between Jewish and Muslim organizations. These encounters were from a grassroots level, to student level, and to high-level encounter, at the level of community leadership. The project's report was launched on 5 July 2005, just two days before the terrible events in London. Understandably, the report was completely overshadowed by coverage of the bombings, and received very little publicity.[1]

The results of the research show that there are frequent contacts between people from Muslim and Jewish backgrounds, people who have found ways of addressing some of the impact of scepticism and extremism to build constructive relationships. The report made a range of recommendations encouraging schools and universities to become more involved in establishing dialogue, and encouraging the use of the arts more imaginatively to create common ground. Many opportunities for dialogue were motivated by efforts to tackle Islamophobia and Antisemitism. This shows how recognizing the disadvantages and discrimination that people face can be a means of identifying common goals. The research findings are heartening given the potential for tensions between communities, and given the expectation of disagreements over foreign policy in relation to Israel.

Muslim Presences and Community Relationships

The third project I want to flag up looks within the Muslim community itself. In a way it challenges some of the established vocabulary and understanding of what we understand by the term 'community'. We often use the phrase 'Muslim Community' as though it were a single group. But it is probably more intellectually honest to view the Muslim presence in this country as a set of different communities rather than one.

This understanding also challenges some of the existing suppositions around community cohesion, because when we talk of community cohesion, we usually talk of establishing links and relationships between what are seen to be distinct communities. So the Christian community may be one in terms of faith, the Muslim community may be another, whereas in terms of ethnicity the Bangladeshi community may be one community, a local, nearby white community may be another. But how strongly does the term 'community' hold up in any of these contexts?

This is something we need to be very careful with. We have been engaged in a number of projects over the last four or five years within Muslim communities, grassroots projects trying to create discussions around issues like Muslim identity, loyalty, belonging, citizenship and so on. We found that there is such a level of diversity and such a level of difference around these notions that they do challenge the term 'community'. In response to this finding, our project brings together a number of different Muslim youth groups from across a wide sectarian spectrum. Surprisingly this has never happened before, or at least not in any sustainable way. Whenever a Muslim organization is talked of, it's usually within quite narrowly defined boundaries; usually sectarian boundaries or class boundaries. What we are trying to do is bring together a very wide range of groups, and it will be quite a challenge to manage the discussion in the group, but an exciting opportunity for people too.

Suggesting that communities are static and can be narrowly defined ignores the diversity within them. Policies aimed at building relationships between supposedly monolithic communities will inevitably fail as they will not relate to many people's conceptions of their own identity or be recognizable to them as a dialogue that includes their community. While there are projects aimed at building relationships between communities – viewed as identifying with large ethnic, or faith-based categories – there must also be some effort to enable communities to develop themselves; to create spaces for dialogue within broader communities.

I hope these three projects give a flavour of the activities that we are conducting in this area.

What Impacts on Identity Formation

Turning to focus on some of the major external factors in Muslim identity formation today I think there are three contemporary, rather negative, issues that have a big effect: (i) foreign policy, (ii) social exclusion, and (iii) Islamophobia, or perceptions of all three – they are not always real. On a contemporary positive or neutral scale there are (a) theological resources as well as (b) parental culture and (c) the wider British culture around us. These I think of as being fundamental, shaping influences or factors. There are two historical points as well: (a) the encounter with colonialism and post-colonial movements, and (b) reactions to the fall of the Caliphate in 1924 and the restorationist movements that tried to re-establish some sort of Muslim political entity. To me each one of these is a major defining factor in the formation of contemporary Muslim identity.

One of the things that really strikes me is that for a Muslim growing up in Britain today, a second- or third-generation British Muslim, most of the external influencing factors are overtly political and based on negative events, e.g. the Iranian Revolution, the Rushdie affair, Bosnia, Algeria, the Gulf War, 9/11 and so on. I fear this has led to identities being skewed in a strongly politicized direction. This has only been exacerbated by the identity politics of Muslim community protests in more recent years. In the wake of this, Muslims are now trying to negotiate with government and the world around. There are many complex factors that need unpacking, but foreign policy is clearly one of them.

Yet there are other influencing factors that are often left out of our discussions. I think there would be benefits from better understanding the sense of everyday lived practice. The majority of people are fundamentally affected by their locality. Yes, they do retain connections with their country of origin which can be very active – travelling backwards and forwards, contacting people in other countries, etc. – but fundamental to most migrant people's experience, particularly those whose families were actually born and brought up in Britain, is where they live.

If you mapped people from the time they got up in the morning to the time they went to bed and looked at their practices, I think a lot of the debate we're having would be re-cast because where they are is what they are living. Whether it's Leicester, Birmingham, London, wherever it is, the fundamental material of existence is rooted in what people do every day. One example struck me a few years ago. Walking down Whitechapel Road on a Friday afternoon when young worshippers were coming out of the mosques, I noticed that all these young guys with some markers of Muslim identity were mainly dressed in trainers and jeans, and looked like any other eastender. They got into cars with loud music, they walked, and they talked like eastenders. Even for those who might try and appropriate an identity that is very traditional in practice, they can't escape the material, which is the clothing, the music, and even the mannerisms. We need more exposure of how people live their daily lives, which is in fact remarkably 'integrated'. What we don't need is for people like David Blunkett and others, after the riots, to say that people need to learn English, when the rioters were most likely communicating in Yorkshire accents – there's something really wrong there.

In terms of community divisions around current debates and internal critiques of certain responses, I think the Muslim community is at a stage where it's only beginning to address some of these issues. It's at least twenty years behind established race discourse, and the debate is nowhere near as sophisticated as the race discourse is today. We don't yet have the giants like Stuart Hall and other such theorists. People are only now emerging who can begin to approach some of those issues from a specifically Muslim perspective. Lack of education and training is a significant factor among Muslim communities and therefore there is a clear polarization between those who go to university, become graduates and go on to do well, and the bulk of the Muslim community who don't make it past GCSE-level education. In this context, to filter back debates that happen amongst academics within this community to the mainstream Muslim communities is a very difficult process. We haven't been able to crack this so far.

Despite what I've said about foreign policy and the globalized aspect of Muslim identity formation, there is a growing impact of the local. Our research shows that there are layers of identity involved. While some

Muslims may not be very comfortably English, they often show strong local identities: being a Brummie, a Londoner or a Scouser, and take pride in being British. Multiple levels of identity are involved here. Sometimes we try to say to people obsessed with foreign affairs – hold on, that's one issue you're interested in, there are others, local social policy issues for example, that your immediate community faces, and that you can change much more easily than foreign policy matters!

There is a gradual move towards Britishness. I think it was Madeleine Bunting who wrote in one of her articles about the London bombings that this wasn't a sign of lack of Britishness. Perhaps it was actually part of the pangs of integration, which need not always be a passive process. And the same goes for the riots. Of course, there were some very terrible repercussions and effects, but we have to acknowledge that these are highly complex issues and we can't solve them with simple solutions. Some of the policy solutions suggested in response are not going to resolve such a complex underlying dynamic.

Note

1   *A Mapping Report of Positive Contact between British Muslims and British Jews* (July 2005, Alif-Aleph UK) is available from the Stone-Ashdown Foundation [www. aauk.org].

5

Policy, Identity and Community Cohesion: How Race Equality Fits

Omar Khan
The Runnymede Trust

Providing linkages between policies and concepts is a difficult enterprise but one that is necessary for justifying and ultimately evaluating the implementation of government measures. A good way of foregrounding the importance of concepts in justifying policy is by asking the related questions: Who benefits? And what benefits do they receive? In relation to the key terms of this volume, it may be tempting to respond by answering that the beneficiaries are various identity groups, and that the benefit they receive is increased community cohesion. However, the simplicity of such a response belies the difficulty not only for the concepts in question – as we go on to argue – but does not focus adequately on how other important principles influence and indeed constrain the capacity of these concepts to impact directly on government policy.

In this chapter we focus on how race equality is one such principle. In the process we aim to provide guidance on how identity and community cohesion can inform government policy while at the same time the commitment to equal consideration and respect – especially for those members of disadvantaged communities – remains fundamental. But first we consider how current government policies interpret and link these concepts within the rubric of larger policy frameworks (whether or not they do so consciously).

Government Agendas: Choice and Respect

Two of the overarching agendas employed by the government to explain and justify current policy initiatives are 'choice' and 'respect'. In particular, the Labour government has emphasized that its reforms in health, education and housing are about giving patients, parents and residents choice in how these important services are provided to them. The idea is that because individuals are typically better placed to understand their own particular needs and interests, it makes sense to provide them with 'choice' even in frontline public services.[1]

How does this emphasis on 'choice' link to the question of identity or indeed community cohesion? It is often argued that the various communities to which we belong help shape if not define our various preferences and indeed our needs (see Kymlicka, 1989; and Margalit and Raz, 1994; for the classic expositions of these views). If this is indeed the case, then our 'identity' will, at least in part, be determined by the communities to which we belong, with all their ethnic, cultural and religious ties. Taking this view of community, policies such as the extension of faith schools are justified because they maximize the choices for people with different identities, namely those with different religious beliefs. A serious difficulty with this view is that it assumes communities to be so static and sharply defined that our choices flow clearly and consistently from identities defined in this way. It also doesn't allow us to evaluate the sorts of choices that people make, some of which may directly harm themselves or others, including their children (Brighouse and Swift, 2006).

Alongside 'choice' as the most prominent policy framework for the current Labour government, the idea of 'respect' is invoked to justify a wide range of measures. For example, anti-social behaviour orders (ASBOs) are recommended largely because perpetrators of certain sorts of acts are regarded as being deficient in the quality of 'respect';[2] such young individuals then undermine community cohesion because of their failure to respect the needs and interests of their fellow citizens. If citizens need to exhibit respect for each other, and if our various communities are important to our identity, it follows that support for community organizations can be not only a way of strengthening people's identities but of furthering respect between all citizens (Taylor, 1994).

The Role and Aim of Policy in Identity

It is not so easy to link these two most important planks of the current government agenda to the meaning and value of identity and community cohesion. This is partly because the government does not ordinarily use the term 'identity', but also because there are tensions between some influential interpretations of the concepts 'identity' and 'community cohesion'. While most academic researchers (including the contributors to this volume) generally support a reasonably fluid conception of identity, government policy seems based on more fixed notions of the various communities that exist in Britain today.

This is partly understandable because it allows for more straightforward design and implementation of policy – although difficulties remain in terms of the relationship between fixed identities and other principles such as fairness and equality. If we were to reject fixed conceptions of identity in favour of their fluid attributes, it becomes harder to determine the nature and the form of the various public policies we might adopt. It also becomes more of a struggle to support the values that underpin a race equality agenda when more and more effort has to be devoted to acknowledging and showing consideration for the sometimes contradictory claims of multifarious forms of identity.

According to an increasingly popular understanding, identity and community cohesion represent two divergent ways of responding to difference, and in particular ethnic and cultural diversity. For many commentators 'identity' suggests a model of society made up of discrete and coherent communities where the maintenance of their distinctiveness becomes a legitimate aim of government policy. On the other hand, 'community cohesion' implies a more holistic if not inflexible understanding of society with the integration of all individuals and communities the ultimate aim of policy measures. This distinction seems particularly central in the interpretation and prominence given to the 'disturbances' that occurred in Bradford, Burnley and Oldham over five years ago, where people's separate identities were diagnosed as the illness, and community cohesion prescribed as the cure (Home Office, 2001, better known as the Cantle report).[3]

This identity/community cohesion distinction is rejected by most researchers, despite its resonance in parts of the media. In particular, the conceptualization of key terms is too rigid in both cases. As Brah characteristically argues in the case of identity:

> identity is not an already given thing but rather it is a process. It is not something fixed that we carry around with ourselves like a piece of luggage. Rather, it is constituted and changes with changing contexts. It is articulated and expressed through identifications within and across different discourses. (Brah, this volume, p. 143)

If identity is fluid, in process and relational, it obviously cannot be linked to what critics see as multiculturalism's pernicious fallout: 'parallel lives'. At the same time, consider some of the consequences of the more 'fixed' notions of identity that characterize current government policy, especially including those measures linked to the 'choice' and 'respect' agendas.

When faith schools are suggested as a way of responding to the needs and particular choices of Muslim (or Christian, Hindu, Jewish, etc.) parents, the identity of the Muslim community is taken as known and relatively fixed. But there may well be Muslim parents (and, more to the point, Muslim children) who would rather have or be better off with well-resourced, non-faith-based schools in their area. Unlike their more religiously oriented co-members, such individuals do not see their 'choices' or 'identity' become a justification of government policy. Does this mean that they are shown less 'respect' as a person because their identity and indeed their choices are ignored while other viewpoints are 'celebrated'? It may be far less obvious to construct policy on the basis of the more fluid conceptions of identity than on static ones, but if identity is going to be useful for policy, it cannot be interpreted in such a selective fashion (Appiah, 2005).

Community Cohesion in Policy

Similarly, community cohesion, however represented in government policy, is also interpreted quite differently by various observers.[4] A number of values have been suggested as providing the 'glue' or principles of community cohesion, and even the Cantle report had difficulty defining it precisely. While it offered 'common values and a civic culture', 'social order and social control', 'social solidarity and reductions in wealth disparities', 'social networks and social capital', and 'place attachment and identity' as 'domains' of community cohesion in the main text of the report, this laundry list was further extended in Appendix C of the document (Home Office, 2001: 13 and 69–75). It is far from clear which of these senses of community cohesion dominates current government thinking. The race equality strategy 'Improving Opportunity, Strengthening Society' (IOSS) emphasizes both political and more overtly cultural forms of community (Home Office, 2005a). While this includes an emphasis on 'Britishness', the document stresses the need for the concept to be 'inclusive'. In sum, the document again emphasizes the multiple interpretations presented in the Cantle report.

However, the various interpretations of community cohesion cannot always easily and happily coexist, a dilemma explored throughout this chapter. This can be seen in IOSS whose commitment to a better society is somewhat undermined by a tendency to conceptualize opportunities, cohesion and combating racism as three separate aims. This tendency is reinforced where the government has separate targets and beneficiaries for enhancing opportunities, increasing cohesion and isolating racists. A good example of this problem is the document's view of racism in terms of the 'disease model': only a few individuals in society are afflicted with the disease and if we quarantine or treat them then the phenomenon will disappear. But racism affects all sorts of institutions and organizations and is more insidious and wide-ranging than the disease model implies. In this same context the lack of discussion of 'institutional racism' is notable.[5] In general, government documents do not explore at length how various concepts – say cohesion and anti-racism – can come into conflict. Instead it parses out certain goals in the hope of avoiding them.

But let's consider here what can emerge when the meaning and scope of 'identity' is considered in combination with community cohesion. If

IOSS does not pursue this line because it does not consider the concept of 'identity', it is worth trying to say something more about how identity and community cohesion can be interpreted so that potential conflicts are mitigated. This allows us to respond coherently and consistently not only to the disadvantage faced by minority ethnic groups in Britain but also to some of the social and political problems facing every citizen. Indeed, the concept of 'identity' is implicitly invoked by government in a particular sort of response by the Labour party to one of its most immediate concerns: the loss in support from white working class Britons.

Labour and the White Working Class

Margaret Hodge's controversial observations on increasing BNP support among the white working class in her east London constituency demonstrated that many in the Labour party are worried about what they perceive to be declining support from their historic base.[6] The political significance of this concern is that many have responded by emphasizing cultural traditions the BNP is deemed to have tapped into effectively So, for example, there are suggestions to 'reclaim' St George's flag and to listen more carefully to the interests and demands of white working-class Britons, a concern that can be described as paying attention to their identity.

This interpretation gains plausibility when multiculturalism and 'identity politics' are heavily censured. Here the assumption is that multiculturalism has *caused* current levels of residential segregation as well as animosity between white and non-white Britons, particularly in terms of access to public housing. Whereas minority ethnic residents are now given enhanced respect and resources (so the story goes), the white working class find their culture undermined and so experience their identity as being under threat. For some government officials and other commentators, multiculturalism in particular is seen to be responsible for creating ethnic segregation by concentrating on how to support particularistic identities (Phillips, 2005).[7]

While it is undoubtedly true that a combination of decreased job opportunities in manufacturing (from 7 million in 1975 to 3 million today) and increased pressures on public housing provision have intensified vulnerability among the white working class, it is disingenuous to pin all the blame on multiculturalism. In fact, residential segregation predates multiculturalist policies. What is new is the tendency to view structural disadvantage in cultural or identity-based terms, not simply among minority ethnic communities but for the white working class as well.

This is not to criticize the view that there are white working-class cultures and identities. It is more to point out that, when they are endorsed by the Labour party, it is from the viewpoint that cultural concerns – the ones some seem to think the BNP has tapped into – need to motivate policy. While many identity-based viewpoints can and will be entirely faultless, and a number will be positively contributory, some may run contrary to the interests of others in society, among them the already unjustly disadvantaged such as minority ethnic groups, women and gays. Furthermore, we must recall the warnings of Brah and others that identity is not fixed. What it means to be white working class today in one region is very different from what it did and might mean elsewhere at a different moment in time. Those who turn to a simplistic understanding of community cohesion as a response to the various needs, interests and identities in Britain today should bear this in mind.

At the same time political parties are losing their obvious affiliation with a particular class or classes. Indeed, many have argued that political parties have moved away from programmatic visions and instead use the views of focus groups to determine policy on the basis of little more than numbers and percentages. Even if such a view is too sweeping, Labour's relative failure to improve the life chances of what historically was its primary support base, the working class, means that its critical analysis of the policies it ought to pursue has no consistently identifiable basis. Especially in public comments by ministers, the government is as likely to focus on 'identity' issues, whether based on specific working-class traditions or not, as it is to demand greater investment in public housing, job training or indeed income transfers.

Working-class identities (just as minority ethnic identities) are not mere inventions and have a real role in alleviating patterned disadvantage. But the demand to eliminate *all* forms of unjust disadvantage needs to reiterated, and this is an aim that cannot be achieved simply by surveying the various identities in Britain and attempting to craft different policies for the different results. Responding to the specific needs of different individuals and communities is important because inequality and disadvantage are typically patterned. They require different forms of intervention in order to be successful. What some in government view as contributing to separatism may in fact contribute to increased confidence, from which can spring community cohesion, when it's interpreted in a more reciprocal and inclusive way.

Paradigms that appear to be good or effective ways of responding to political dilemmas can't always straightforwardly go together – an observation not limited to Labour's policies or those of any other political party. Beyond this observation, and to say something about the justification of policies more broadly, we shall here try to chart a way of understanding policies in general that provides a framework for interpreting the relationship between identity, community cohesion and race equality.

Policies as a Means to an End

> The cause of integration has become so fetishised since the July bombings that it has been elevated to the level of an intrinsic moral value – not a means to an end but an end in itself. (Younge, 2005)

Policies are simply a means of pursuing a certain aim. In many circumstances, the aims are either too abstract or simply impossible to achieve directly. Take, for example, 'good race relations' or 'equal opportunities'. Even if we assume agreement on the meaning and benefit of these aims, it is not always clear what policies we might adopt. Indeed different democracies have developed different policy measures in both these areas. One of the greatest difficulties for a government is to be explicit about the principles underlying a policy while in the same breath emphasizing the policy's importance in achieving real-world benefits. When a certain policy fails to meet its objective, say through poor implementation rather than a weak principle, this difficulty is compounded – do you then have to jettison the principle along with the failed policy?

But when the meaning of such aims is as capacious (and varied) as those of identity and community cohesion, further concerns emerge. For example, if we disagree about the meaning of an aim, we are likely to disagree about whether a particular policy did or did not achieve it. In the case of identity the problem is compounded by the fact that its content and indeed its benefits are in many ways psychological in nature, and not easily perceived as deriving from a government policy. The same might be said of community cohesion, especially when the emphasis is on its local forms, or when the government aims to provide its citizens with something as elusive as a 'sense of belonging' (see IOSS).

It is therefore necessary to be clearer about the particular conceptions of identity and community cohesion we have in mind, or in other words to be clearer about what they aim to achieve. For Runnymede, the goal in both instances is *the equal participation of all citizens in British life*. We attend to the importance people find in their identities because it is extremely likely that these affect their capacity to participate in society as equals and indeed for institutions to be fair. However, given the importance of race equality (and indeed democracy), such identities must not be contradictory to basic precepts of tolerance and fairness. Community cohesion, on the other hand, contributes to fair institutions and a society where all participate as equals only if the concept is understood in a *progressive* way: societies may be cohesive but also exclusionary and repressive. In order to explain this further, we examine some of the key concepts, in particular by exploring the links between them and other research trends.

Social Capital – Bonding and Bridging

A common framework for distinguishing forms of community interaction can be found in the social capital literature, where a distinction is made between 'bonding' and 'bridging' social capital (Putnam, 2000; Varshney, 2003). While the former explains social ties *within* a particular community or groups, the latter focuses on social ties *across* various social groups. Whatever the weaknesses of the social capital approach, it is worth examining how this distinction bears on the questions of identity, community cohesion and ethnic diversity, particularly when the government is keen on using this framework to explain its policy goals (CFMEB, 2000; Runnymede, 2005; World Bank, n.d.).[8]

While both bonding and bridging social capital have undoubted strengths for individuals and society at large, there are also dilemmas for each of these networks. For example, bonding social capital can work to exclude people; even those who draw strength and support from their existing social networks recognize the potential problems for such networks where they place constraints on group members. More positively, the creation of bonding social capital within disadvantaged communities can be an important way to provide them with necessary resources and eventually allow them to participate with more confidence in public life. Given the state's interest in the equal participation of all, this is a potential reason for government to support such bonding social capital.

Yet recently it has become popular to call for a rejection of multiculturalist policies on the basis that there has been too much concentration on bonding and not enough emphasis on bridging social capital. According to such a view, 'In recent years we've focused far too much on the "multi" and not enough on the common culture. We've emphasized what divides us over what unites us. We have allowed tolerance of diversity to harden into the effective isolation of communities, in which some people think special separate values ought to apply' (Phillips, 2005). This line from the Chair of the Commission on Racial Equality echoes a common theme of government, the opposition and much of the media, but is questionable on both empirical and normative grounds.

Empirically, it is not at all obvious that multiculturalism *caused* residential segregation, a relatively long-term phenomenon not simply in Britain but experienced by migrants throughout the world who often come from similar towns or regions, work in specific industries and build networks of support in order to meet basic needs, and who often live together to provide each other with a sense of security.[9] Normatively, if certain citizens are *not* being included in British life to the extent that this disadvantages them, it is counterintuitive if not obtuse to suggest that they desire to live unequal and less fulfilling lives. It is far more likely that those who seek social ties among their fellow group members do so because they feel unable to participate in institutions of power, and discriminated against by those who claim to include them.

This goes to the heart of the debate about segregation, a debate in which causal claims are rarely backed up by good empirical data. For critics of multiculturalism, it sometimes appears as if disadvantaged individuals are self-consciously striving to exclude themselves, and too little mention is made of the responsibility of the state for ensuring equal participation or indeed its role in reducing economic disparities. In this context, it is notable that 'institutional racism', so prominent in the Stephen Lawrence Inquiry report (Macpherson, 1999), is rarely mentioned as part of the problem. While it is of course important to design appropriate policy in response to segregation in our cities, it is singularly unhelpful to assume it has been caused solely by multiculturalism and to deflect responsibility from the state's other actions (and inactions).

If critics are right that we have been encouraging separatism, we might expect more diverse areas to have high levels of bonding social capital (concentrating on 'what divides us') and low levels of bridging social capital (ignoring 'what unites us'). Instead, evidence suggests that more diverse areas have low levels of bonding social capital *as well as* low levels of bridging social capital. Despite the accusations, multiculturalist policies – to the extent that they have been pursued comprehensively – have failed even to create greater bonding social capital. As recognized at least since the work of Gordon Allport, and pursued in countless works over the past 50 years, what matters is not simply the quantity of interactions we have with people of different backgrounds, but the *quality* of those interactions (Allport, 1954; Hewstone et al., 2005; also represented in this volume by Hewstone et al.).

A good way to understand the potential benefits of bonding social capital is that it can create confidence and encourage the participation of those who are not represented in or by institutions of power. Of course we should discourage people from shutting off completely from others, but this often presents the empirical case back to front: people foster social links with each other when other institutions, including the state, fail to provide them with services that allow them to participate as equals. If creating or fostering identities is seen as a key plank in creating engaged citizens, or in fostering 'bonding' social capital, then government has a reason to intervene in helping construct or support identities. It is a legitimate aim too, but only where that identity is supported in order to give disadvantaged citizens the confidence and resources to participate more widely.

From Identities to Cohesion?

A slightly different way of interpreting the value of community identities is that creating or fostering such identities (bonding social capital) is a *means* to community cohesion. On this reading, community cohesion and not identity is the *aim* of government. This is because identities are perceived as necessary for community cohesion but perhaps not valuable in themselves. There are a number of difficulties for such an interpretation, not least because it privileges certain types of identities (which are in turn perceived to be static and monolithic) and because it is not at all clear that community cohesion is a desirable aim regardless of how that 'cohesion' comes about.

But one undoubted strength of viewing policies that relate to identity as achieving some alternative aim is that it permits the distinction between narrow exclusionary forms of identity and those that are expansive and progressive. Those who have clear notions of their identity, Protestants or Catholics in Northern Ireland for example, are not always or even often likely to have a high level of civic participation (e.g. Khan, 2006a). However, a principled distinction between narrow and progressive forms of identities in any government policy must announce its alternative aims clearly. For us at Runnymede, the equalities and human rights agendas provide the backdrop against which we attempt to assess any government policy measure for its intrinsic fairness. This brings us to the much-debated topic of 'Britishness'.

On Britishness

In an article in *Prospect*, David Goodhart initiated a contentious debate about the value of 'Britishness' in contributing to a sense of solidarity. This view might not seem incompatible with putting support for human rights and equality at the forefront of a progressive understanding of identity, cohesion and race equality, but we are sceptical that the concept of 'Britishness' can provide much support or justification for government policy, especially in the case of identity and equality. As Bhikhu Parekh's response to Goodhart expresses it:

> Goodhart talks of British 'ideals,' but does not say what these are… and whether there is or can be a national consensus on them. He talks of a coherent national story, preferably a Whiggish view of national history. But this is only one story among several. Tories won't share it, and nor would immigrants and the radical left because of its failure to offer a balanced account of the British empire. He wants our identity to be defined in cultural rather than political terms as is the case today, but does not say what that involves and whether it is not likely to be too exclusive to accommodate legitimate diversity … He talks of 'Britishness' as if being British is not a relational category signifying mutual commitment but a quality, like redness or sweetness, that all British people must uniformly share. (Parekh, 2006)

What is truly important about forms of solidarity or cohesion is that they should be progressive, by which we mean that they embody, both now and into the future, the value of equal concern and respect for all. The issue is therefore not 'Britishness' but of ensuring that 'cohesion' is truly progressive. Although it is indeed true that partiality towards co-nationals inspires great sacrifices, it is important to recognize that this need not be the same sort of regard for others as a commitment to justice, a commitment that ultimately derives from being a part of shared political and social institutions. I see no reason to believe that those who are most concerned to discharge their obligations to their co-nationals will be those most likely to be committed to the value of distributive fairness within a schema of shared cooperation (or even to share resources with their co-nationals). As Arthur Ripstein puts it 'I mean only to question the claim that readiness to make one sort of sacrifice tells us very much about readiness to make others' (Ripstein, 1997: 216).

Government can opt to finesse this question by handing down its own definition of Britishness as wholly positive and progressive and by linking it with abstract concepts such as freedom, equality and fairness – as suggested by Gordon Brown, Ruth Kelly and others (Brown, 2006; Kelly, 2006). However politically astute such a linkage may be, it suggests the implausible consequence that progressives from other countries can be exhibiting Britishness, while those Britons who fail to treat their fellow citizens fairly or support redistributive taxation are somehow 'unBritish'.

Surely it is better to spell out the principles that should guide government policy and recommend these principles for their contribution to a better and fairer society where all individuals are treated with equal concern and respect. If people identify this as part of what it means to be British, so much the better. For those who think that human rights are not part of being British, we must show them why they are wrong historically (which we think they are), and if that fails to convince them, then what it means to be British must be made to accommodate such central values. But in any case this means that we do think important principles are non-negotiable, so much so that we don't want to base them on the vagaries of what it means to be British.

Political Equality and Equal Respect

A central concern for the contributors to this volume is the particular difficulty of speaking about political engagement in terms of identity, particularly when trying to interpret it in policy terms. Although the distinction between public and private has taken a bit of a battering, and is fuzzier than originally thought, there are good reasons to assume that certain areas of social and personal life ought not to be subject to direct government interference. We therefore emphasize *public* concerns in questions of policy. Whatever the vagueness of their distinction from private concerns, and even if the effects of government decisions extend widely into social life, government policy is ordinarily and best conceived to be most legitimate when it deals with issues of public concern and when limited in the scope of its intervention.

How does the wider society – and political institutions in particular – treat citizens? The key justificatory aim of policies that foster identities is to enhance equal concern and respect, or to ensure that all citizens are treated fairly by key political and social institutions (Rawls, 1971).[10] This is central to an equalities and human rights agenda and indeed part of the meaning of justice and political liberty. Where there is patterned disadvantage, it is difficult if not impossible for members of some groups to achieve the standing required for them participate as equals in public institutions and public debate. Inequalities in the private sphere are usually implicated in reduced participation, and so may be considered legitimate targets for government policymaking where relevant. In a democracy, it is important in all aspects of policymaking not to lose sight of the supreme value of fairness and participation in public institutions.

How do policies achieve a given aim? Simply identifying an aim, even one as foundational as equal concern and respect or fairness in government institutions, does not imply that people must always be treated exactly *the same*. So, for example, even a policy of quotas does not obviously fall foul of the aim of making society fairer if all members of a certain group, say Untouchables in India or Blacks in South Africa, are comprehensively discriminated against and so denied the opportunity to participate as equals (see Khan, 2006b, for an extended argument along these lines). There is an important empirical question about whether or not such circumstances exist, but it is possible that the only way to achieve fairness in the broadest sense is to treat some individuals preferentially. A way of formalizing this thought is as follows:

A should be equal to B in terms of X (public participation);
and so
A should be treated preferentially to B in terms of Y (jobs or places).

Here 'Y' is not itself an end, but the only or perhaps the most effective means of achieving the aim, specified as 'X' (see Khan, 2006b, on the putative difference between affirmative action and 'universal' policies). Or, as Ronald Dworkin has famously put it, the point is to treat people as equals, even if that sometimes means people are treated differentially (Dworkin, 1978).

Back to Identity?

What does the notion of preferential treatment have to do with identity? Consider the proposition that individuals need to feel sufficient dignity in order to engage in public debate or indeed to participate in or access public institutions more broadly. As most of us recognize, there is both a self-directed and other-directed form of this respect. Part of my self-esteem is based on my own psychological and social resources, but part of it is determined by how others see me. And if everyone (or almost everyone) in dominant groups views people like me as being unworthy of respect then I will be incapable of participating.

This problem is particularly difficult for public institutions, whose very logic often requires being 'blind' to the various differences between citizens in order to treat them fairly. For this to be possible, individuals must be confident that people who share relevant aspects of their identity are in fact treated fairly and represented in public institutions and in public debate. In so far as supporting certain types of 'community organizations' helps give individuals the confidence to participate, government policy in this area will be justifiable.

Some will interpret this as providing support for a free-for-all fragmentation of society where individuals see themselves first as having identities and commitment to narrower communities. This is a surprisingly common error. One way of conceptualizing the justification of such policies is through Parekh's interpretation of multiculturalism as 'interactive, dialogical or pluralist':

> Multiculturalism in this sense is open, interactive, dynamic and creative. Its main policy concern is to create conditions and devise programmes such that different cultural communities feel valued and respected, are *integrated* in appropriate ways, and interact *within an agreed system of rights and obligations*. (Parekh, this volume, p.131, emphasis added)

In this chapter we are trying to provide further support for this argument by pointing out that programmes like these are ultimately justifiable through their contribution to a truly fair and democratic society, and identity groups need not hinder this fundamental aim. Where they do make a fairer society less likely, we have no objection to denying them government resources.

Citizenship and Progressive Solidarity

At the same time, we think that citizenship is *not* best conceived of in terms of 'identity'. In order for the concept to have any coherence, citizenship must apply to all equally, regardless of their attitude towards the rights and responsibilities that such citizenship confers.[11] People might have different attitudes towards citizenship, but suggesting that citizenship is an identity focuses our attention too much on psychological concerns and implies that it can be differentially or constantly negotiated by different individuals. No-one can sign away their basic rights. Citizenship is more appropriately thought of as a *status* that we either have or we don't. This is not to say that there is no such thing as a 'political identity'; indeed, it is to affirm it by suggesting that one's attitudes to citizenship and ambitions to change or conserve political institutions (perhaps an 'ideological identity') cannot justify the state's denial of basic human rights to all citizens.

We therefore agree with those who argue that societies where people respect one another not only have greater stability and community cohesion, but are also more likely to express support for progressive values because mutual respect contributes to reduced inequalities in power. This is also where the more abstract elements of human rights and equality link to our interpretation of community cohesion: inequalities and rights violations are likely to make individuals, both minority ethnic and white, less able to feel like they are part of a shared project and so less likely to be motivated to share resources. But rather than follow Goodhart in making cultural cohesion the key policy question for increasing people's willingness to cooperate justly, we instead focus on responding to tangible disadvantages, including the lack of opportunities for equal participation for some individuals. Inequalities and reduced participation not only severely undermine 'healthy community life' but a just and functioning democracy.

Identity, Community Cohesion and Runnymede's Ongoing Agenda

Identity research can make an impact on policy by insisting that race equality and human rights values cannot be violated by whatever measures or funding get provided under the heading of 'identity'. However, it is of more than merely academic interest to discover the views and experiences of marginalized groups, especially where these have been ignored in the past, and also where they can be related directly to policy agendas of the present day.

Three recent and ongoing Runnymede research programs are engaged critically with the 'choice' or 'respect' agendas, and in researching the needs of different 'identities' in Britain today. While our analytic intent is to arrive at a point where we understand how these somewhat abstract ideas and policy agendas actually play out in modern Britain, and whereas we try to adopt a neutral perspective (as far as that is possible), we are always guided by the idea that research needs to contribute to building a better society, where values such as equality and fairness extend to all citizens coherently and consistently.

Our work on a number of 'community studies' is beginning to produce reports that endeavour to understand the dynamics of communities in Britain that currently define themselves by ethnicity, especially smaller communities (e.g. Vietnamese, Bolivian) who may have more difficulty in participating equally and having their needs addressed. By working with community-based organizations and enabling a range of voices to define their key political and social topics, we aim to support bonding and bridging social capital and thereby increase their capacity to participate. We also want to highlight changes in the diversity of our society by focusing on communities that are not recognized in the official census. Including these 'identity groups' more widely in public debate is not only good for them, but for the functioning and quality of democracy, and in consequence good for all of us.

In researching schools and ethnic segregation, a topic of particular relevance given the government's 'choice' agenda, our key aim is to consider what influences the choices that parents from Black and minority ethnic communities are making and whether and how they differ from those made by white parents. This study may lead to a better understanding of the motives for segregation, a topic whose capacity to stimulate media interest is not matched by empirical analysis. Through this research we will also consider how and whether structural barriers constrain the choices made by young people from ethnic groups, children who continue to underachieve in our classrooms.

In an allied project, and again exploring the meaning and contours of 'choice', we are investigating the impact that faith schools have on community cohesion. To do this, we are creating a learning dialogue between schools to help them consider how they could promote meaningful contact between young people of different faiths (including children of a secular background or disposition). While a controversial debate about the meaning, significance and consequences of extending choice throughout the public services is being maintained, this sort of empirically grounded research can shine a light on the impact of choice on race equality in education. This issue is important not just for minority ethnic parents and children, but crucial for ensuring that all children are brought up in a culture of fairness and tolerance so that they can participate equally as adults.

To ensure that equality remains central to the public policy debates, some of our work focuses on ways in which measures can impact disproportionately on people from certain minority ethnic communities. One example is our study of the effect of the 'respect' agenda on race equality – in particular the increasing use of ASBOs to provide 'community safety'. The key question for this research is: can our local government, policing and housing structures and institutions avoid the racialized outcomes that undermine so many other criminal justice initiatives? (Isal, 2006) Runnymede has also interrogated the proposed far-reaching changes in pensions provision to determine their impact on poverty among Black and minority ethnic pensioners (Runnymede, 2006).[12]

Conclusion: Equalities, Redistribution and Democracy

Runnymede and other equalities-focused organizations are sometimes criticized for emphasizing racial inequalities at the expense of economic analysis. Too many commentators, it seems to us, are insufficiently clear-headed to see that struggling against unjust economic and ethnic inequalities *is* part of a shared agenda. When one commits to reducing inequalities and supporting human rights, it should be obvious that all forms of unjustifiable disadvantage ought to be combated. Partly for this reason, public policies that support community organizations or that otherwise attend to the various identities of different types of Britons can and should be justified on the basis of a shared platform – namely reducing inequalities and redistributing resources, including those of power. This is not simply a matter of expediency, but the best way to justify policies and indeed to create the conditions for a better-functioning and fairer democracy. The alternative is either to ignore certain forms of unjust disadvantage or to claim that some inequalities are less amenable to government intervention. If the first option displays a blinkered moral view, the second is either intellectually lazy or simply dishonest.

Again, it is worth emphasizing that identity research can matter because it contributes to our understanding of the unmet needs of certain (typically disadvantaged) groups, and so contributes to the important aim of equal concern and respect. Support for 'identities' can contribute to this goal by providing everyone with the confidence to participate in institutions of power. And we recognize that 'community cohesion' – or at least a certain reading of it – can contribute to an equality agenda too, not because it is valuable for its own sake but because it can help to create a good society and because it contributes to the welfare (and equal participation) of all. The contingent value of identity[13] and community cohesion is well captured by Amy Gutmann in her insightful book *Identity in Democracy*:

> To describe identity groups in a value neutral way would be to misdescribe and misunderstand not only identity groups but the nature of democracy. Democracies are not neutral political instruments; they are worth defending to the extent that they institutionalize in politics a more ethical treatment of individuals than the political alternatives to democracy, which range from benevolent to malevolent autocracies and oligarchies. Some identity groups aid democracies in institutionalizing more equal treatment of individuals and others impede it. A critical part of a description of the role of identity groups in democracies must therefore be to develop a language that helps us to understand their role in both aiding and impeding the pursuit of democratic justice. (Gutmann, 2003: 27)

We have pointed out how policy design needs to ensure that its aims and consequences are more likely to aid than impede democratic justice. Some might find this naïve or counterproductive or indeed contrary to some of the contributions to this volume, where the 'authentic voice' of certain communities may seem out of step with the vision propounded here.

This is where Gutmann's book provides incisive assistance: she points out that identity groups are neither good nor bad but part of democratic politics, both because the groups to which people belong shape their values and matter to them, and because individuals are far more likely to shape politics through acting with others than acting alone – in a democracy, numbers count. Research into the various 'identity groups' in Britain today is worthwhile because it aims to present fairly and accurately the experiences and views of many different people in society. And this must include research into white communities, especially disadvantaged white communities who also face challenges in participating equally in British life.

For these reasons the Labour party's concern about the white working class is not entirely self-serving, though we would rather see it framed in terms of the effects of powerlessness on public participation than focused on the cultural attractions of the BNP. At the same time, research must not simply be sugar-coated to present only those progressive and democratic tendencies of white or Black and minority ethnic groups; the importance of objective research is independent of whatever policies the government can and ought to pursue.

Here again we would like to return to the question of the link between academic research and policy. There are some who think that organizations like Runnymede should provide a clear programme of action, with explicit policy suggestions, perhaps implying that various independent research organizations should be seen as shadow governments. Not only is this contrary to democratic principles, it fails to consider the way in which research bodies have an interest in principles and ideas as well as practicalities.

When thinking about the impact academic research has on policy, it is not always immediately obvious what conclusions should or might follow. A good way of guiding the development of practical measures is always to invoke matters of principle. This ensures not only that policies are well-crafted but also that our evaluation of their effects is based on their actual contribution to aims that improve human welfare.

In this chapter we have looked at some of the links between identity, community cohesion and minority ethnic disadvantage as understood by government, and suggested why the 'choice' and 'respect' agendas – as currently understood – cannot provide effective or good policy frameworks. Concurrently, and by way of constructing an alternative understanding of these links, we suggest that the important principles of equality and democracy should always guide the development and implementation of policies in these areas, and thereby ensure that they actually benefit all members of our society, especially those from disadvantaged communities.

Notes

1. For an evaluation of this view, see the Public Administration Select Committee's report (2005) and the Government's response (Cabinet Office, 2005).
2. See the *Respect Action Plan* published by the Home Office: http://www.home office.gov.uk/documents/respect-action-plan. See also the 'Respect' website at: http://www.respect.gov.uk/, which has the heading 'Respect cannot be learned, purchased or acquired – it can only be earned'.
3. For more recent variants on this theme, see Shadow Home Secretary David Davis's comments on Muslim 'apartheid' and Tony Blair's intervention on the dismissal of a Muslim teaching assistant for wearing a *niqab*.

4. It is worth revisiting the report of the Commission on the Future of Multi-Ethnic Britain – the Parekh Report (CFMEB, 2000), which provided a definition of cohesion prior to the Cantle report, and prior to the disturbances of 2001 in the northern mill towns, and influenced government thinking at the time. This definition emphasizes deliberative democratic procedures rather than social control or supposedly static identities: 'Cohesion derives from widespread commitment to certain core values, both between communities and within them: equality and fairness; dialogue and consultation; toleration, compromise and accommodation; recognition and respect for diversity; ... and determination to confront and eliminate racism and xenophobia' (p. 56).

5. The unpopularity of the Stephen Lawrence Inquiry report, particularly in certain sections of the media, may explain this shift in discourse.

6. See, e.g., the BBC's coverage of her comments on its website 'Minister says BNP tempting voters' (16 April 2006).

7. This view has since become more popular. See Jack Straw's comments on the *niqab* in October 2006 and David Davis's comments in August 2005 and on 'Muslim apartheid' in October 2006.

8. On the inability of social capital approaches to deal effectively with problems of differential power and structural disadvantage remain, see Fine (2005). One problem for government policy is that bridging capital seems to be associated with middle-class organizations while bonding is stipulated as the preferred course of minority ethnic engagement, an assumption that does not stand up to strict scrutiny.

9. Critics of residential 'segregation' too often forget or simply ignore the fact that migrants and members of minority ethnic communities can be subject to abuse, some of it violent. It is hardly surprising or indeed morally objectionable that people live together in order to ensure their bodily security. Furthermore, for people who have certain dietary requirements, living in an area with better provision of certain foods and spices is again the best way of meeting important needs, not of articulating a sense of separateness.

10. John Rawls has argued that the social conditions required for self-respect should be understood as a 'primary good', by which he means that all citizens in a just democracy require it. Although the argument is complicated, the idea is that the good of self-esteem is achieved where the value of political liberties, including the ability to participate, is equal for all citizens (Rawls, 1971, especially §§ 67 and 82). For many disadvantaged groups in democracies throughout the world, the value of political liberty is not equal, which is why alternative policies need to be considered – not as a question of 'identity', but as a question of justice.

11. This links to an unfortunate error in the government's 'Respect' agenda – namely the misguided thought that respect must be 'earned'. Even convicted criminals and those who throw bricks through windows have a basic dignity or worth that the government cannot deny. Indeed, in order for a democratic government to have legitimacy, it must affirm the equal worth and respect of

all of its citizens, an aim that is obviously hindered by the government's current understanding of the concept of respect.

12.   Full versions of both the ASBO and Pensions papers are available at www. runnymedetrust.org.

13.   For many liberals, there is an important *non-contingent* value to identity, namely the idea that crafting a good life with particular sorts of ends is ethically important to individuals. John Stuart Mill is sometimes ridiculed for having an exaggerated sense of the capacity for individual autonomy, but as Kwame Anthony Appiah (2005) points out, Mill's ethical vision always placed sociability at its heart. In any case, it is not at all clear how this liberal-individualist emphasis on the ethical centrality of personal identity relates to the more sociologically informed way it is used in this volume and in most other commentaries on identity or identity politics.

PART II

IDENTITIES IN COMMUNITY CONTEXTS: FOUR CASE STUDIES

Each of these case studies examines a context in which issues of community cohesion and identity are particularly salient.

6

Welcome to 'Monkey Island':
Identity and Community in Three Norwich Estates

Ben Rogaly and Becky Taylor
Department of Geography, University of Sussex

In the recent history of the welfare state, particular areas have been identified in official documents as 'deprived' (Damer, 1989; Power, 1996; Social Exclusion Unit, 1998). In response to this, the present government has channelled resources through the New Deal for Communities to selected neighbourhoods, including the North Earlham, Larkman and Marlpit (NELM) estates in Norwich. In this chapter we draw on an ongoing piece of research with estate residents to begin to explore questions regarding shifting social and spatial identity practices in the area.[1]

The New Deal for Communities has the idea of 'community' literally 'at the heart' of a 'long term commitment to deliver real change'. 'Community involvement and [community] ownership' are described as key characteristics.[2] Here we suggest that the very idea of 'community' is a construction that does not necessarily reflect how people think about their relations with others in the neighbourhood they live in. This represents the beginning of our analysis of the interrelation between official descriptions of the area as deprived and residents' own social and spatial identity practices.

Investigating the NELM Estates

Owing to increasingly apparent failures or limited successes of various welfare strategies, social policy theory since 1945 has become more and more preoccupied by the issue of implementation. In the UK in particular 'some passion' has gone into the 'top-down/bottom-up debate', typically linked to arguments about the respective roles of central and local government in the determination and implementation of policy (Hill, 1997). Area-based initiatives have a long history dating back to at least the 19th century. However, an important change occurred following the economic restructuring, privatization, and emphasis on individual responsibility that emerged from the late 1970s. This was manifest in a reengagement with ideas of 'deserving' and 'undeserving' poor people and a move away from a universalist to a targeting strategy. New Labour has retained the emphasis on targets (Imrie and Raco, 2003). This change has created its own problems. Singling out particular neighbourhoods as 'problem areas' can itself perpetuate exclusion and distract attention from the causes of poverty (Morrison, 2003; Rogaly et al., 1999); the same can be equally true of targeting social or ethnic groups (Gotovos, 2003; Mosse, 1999).

While our research project aims to examine how policy constructs places, spaces and identity possibilities, we also seek to go further, to reveal how the agencies of estate residents and historical chance have played their part in the creation of the distinct characters of the estates. Individuals are not simply passive recipients of policy: as was said of the estate residents relocated during slum clearance and confirmed in many of our interviews, 'they have retained much of their former rejection of "authority" and an "independence" of thought and action' (Larkman Project Group, 1984).

Social identifications are made, contested and continuously reconstituted through categorization by others, through conscious, even instrumental, choice, and through unconscious group affiliations, including affective solidarities (Brah, 1996; Jenkins, 1996; Shotter, 1984). Identity practices refer to the actions, inactions, words and silences which either reflect the practical consciousness of taken-for-granted identifications, or which intentionally make use of identifications, for example to construct solidarities or assert group-belonging to achieve particular goals (Halfacree and Boyle, 1993, drawing on Giddens, 1986).

In our research we seek to problematize the idea of 'community', particularly as it is propagated in government social policy towards 'community organizations' and 'community cohesion' (McGhee, 2003). For some, community has become 'a governmentalized discourse' – a central means within 'third-way' politics of 'softening the move towards neo-capitalist restructuring' (Delanty, 2003: 87; Rose, 1999). While taking on board the possibility of such interpretations, we do not seek to argue that estate residents feel no sense of identification with others in their neighbourhood. It is also possible that the existence of an artificially constructed 'community' project can help to create a sense of community – as Castells has argued of urban social movements, 'regardless of the explicit achievement of the movement, its very existence produced meaning' (1997: 61).

We set out to explore both the external identity of the estates, and the shifting and multiple social identifications of estate residents over time. It is hoped that this will contribute to understandings of subjectivity and identification among 'poor white communities' in the UK as a whole. Identity practices operate simultaneously across different dimensions. We examine the interaction of ethnic identifications with identifications based on class, gender, generation and place. To the extent that identifications are performed, particular dimensions of identity are likely to be fore-grounded by the same person in different times and places (Okamura, 1981; Rew and Campbell, 1999; Rogaly et al., 2004). Our understanding of identity practices is thus situational as well as relational. Of particular importance in this interdisciplinary research is analysis of how ideas of place change over time, and of the juxtaposition between the speeds of change in individual identifications and of change in surrounding insti-tutions, buildings, policies and investments (Wolch and DeVerteuil, 2001).

We understand places as 'open, porous and the products of other places' (Massey, 1995: 59). Therefore we locate the estates in relation to their marginal geographical and social position within Norwich, which itself is in the geographical, cultural and social centre of Norfolk, indicat-ing that even the centre has its own margins. When the estates were first constructed they were on the geographical periphery of the city. This physical marginalization was reinforced by the fact that many ex-slum dwellers were rehoused there, resulting in social stigma (Larkman Project Group, 1984; Sibley, 1995). Since that time, the city has expanded beyond the estates, separating them from the surrounding countryside while tying them closer to the city, and meanwhile the University of East Anglia has been built on their doorstep.

At the same time, the social location of the NELM area has undergone profound changes. As well as containing people's homes and neighbour-hoods, its council houses and estates are physical embodiments of the changing face of the welfare state – from council tenancy to the right to buy, to the recent increase in housing association properties (Forrest and Murie, 1991). People's identifications are profoundly tied to their rela-tionship with their houses and the places where they are located (Bornat, 1989; Sixsmith, 1988). Residents' identifications are also meshed with life-cycle patterns. Generational shifts change the patterns of expectation, needs and experiences of individuals in their relationships with their homes and neighbourhood. They also increase diversity within and between households – 'time increases complexity, complexity in turn implies a multiplicity and a plurality of viewpoints' (Strathern, 1992: 21).

At the time of writing this chapter we have conducted taped inter-views with close on 60 individuals, most of them estate residents, and carried out ethnographic work, kept fieldnotes and collected data from national and local archives. This process of data collection is ongoing, and systematic analysis of interview transcripts has not yet begun, so this paper represents a pause, a time for reflection and a refinement of some of our research questions, rather than a presentation of research 'find-ings'. We have spoken to a diverse range of people, young and old, male and female, long-term residents, those who have only recently come to live on the estates and former residents, including some who have returned.

The grey literature we consulted about the estates and our interactions with the NELM New Deal for Communities Partnership had led us to believe that people's spatial and social identifications in the area had a degree of boundedness. Thus there would be 'Travellers', people with Irish heritage and people who had moved to the area from tied cottages in the countryside and from slum clearance in central Norwich. The three estates would relate to clearly understood places, and, because of a history of conflict between the estates, belonging to one of these places would define social relationships with people from each of the other two.

In practice, social and spatial identities are being revealed as even more dynamic and contingent than we had supposed. In what follows we draw on interview data to illustrate how different residents negotiated the insider–outsider divide, how situated identity practices led the boundaries of individual estates to shift, and how histories of movement of people, ideas and capital into and away from the estates have influenced identification and social change. The final section of the paper builds on these emerging insights by raising questions for our ongoing data collection and analysis, as well as for government, regarding the centrality of 'community' in its strategies for long-term change in 'deprived' areas.

Belonging and Community

The NELM New Deal project has actively engaged a relatively small group of people, many with long histories in the area and extended family who are resident on one of the estates or nearby. This group of people, which includes board members and NELM staff, have given up their time to talk to us and have given us contacts with other current and former residents. We have also sought to meet people through other means, for example through social clubs and churches and discussions with people known to us prior to the research, who either live on one of the estates or have been involved there through previous residence or work. Both of us have connections with the area, having lived, worked and/or studied nearby for several years. Being present on the estates over a period of several months, and following these and other routes, has enabled us to speak with recently arrived residents, people who once lived in the area, who left and then returned, as well as with former residents.

Some long-term resident interviewees talked of physical neighbourliness, for example exchange through shopping, or care of houses and pets when a householder was away. To emphasize this point, more than one person cited cases from media reports of other places where elderly people had died in their own homes and not been found for weeks, countering with a remark such as, 'at least round here someone would notice something was wrong'. It was physical support that caused one former resident, who had moved away but continued to work in the area, to seek to move back. As part of her work she had organized a meeting on one of the estates between a Norwich City Council housing officer and estate residents:

> *the other workers in the council have absolutely no idea of the real intense feelings that, that people who can't get their repairs done, actually build up and I just collapsed in the middle of this meeting. The next thing I remember is being in the Norfolk and Norwich [hospital], but apparently it was the locals – the housing office couldn't cope at all – who called an ambulance. It was three members of [names a group of residents] that went up to the hospital, followed the ambulance, stayed with me until four o'clock in the morning ... finding out kind of like what was going to happen. Somebody else took my car keys out of my pocket and drove my car back to their house and parked it up on their garden so that it wouldn't be vandalized ... They totally looked after me ... I was very, very touched and all the while I was in the hospital people kept in touch, sent cards and ... it's one of the reasons I ... moved back to the area.*
> (interviewee 47, 9.01.06)

However, the importance of relations with others on the estate goes beyond neighbourliness to a less specific but nonetheless important feeling of 'belonging'. For many long-term residents the feeling of belonging is about 'knowing everyone', and being part of a web of family networks extending back three or more generations. This point was tellingly illustrated during the course of the fieldwork, when one of us came across two of our interviewees – one in their late 60s, the other in their 30s – in the local café, talking about a recent car accident in which three teenagers were seriously injured. We had been unaware that these two individuals knew each other socially, and the younger woman was attempting to describe the victims of the crash, whose families had once lived on the estate, but no longer did so. In the course of the 10-minute conversation on the subject they talked about the teenagers in terms of their respective families, stretching back to three generations, discussed where they had lived on the estate, their neighbours, and their reputation. Although the older resident did not know the teenagers personally, by the end of the conversation she had located them in the web of relationships that existed across the estates and beyond.

One resident, born on one of the estates and long involved as a member of the NELM staff, vividly expressed his strong sense of belonging to the area as a youth. He described walking back into the estate as 'going into someone's house you, kind of go through the door and the doors shut, you felt secure all the way along the road, you knew all the neighbours, by "auntie" and "uncle" and, you knew, they were all looking out [for you]' (interviewee 15, 4.10.05).

Being known translates for some into a feeling of physical security. This allows other, older residents to feel comfortable walking up to the shops in the dark, as they rationalized that they had known the teenagers since they were babies, and had known their parents before them. In still other cases it engenders a sense of control, and the possibility of being able to confront some of the more threatening parts of life on the estates on equal terms:

we did think about moving right away ... but then because my old man's lived here all his life as well, you see and we sort of thought about it and, there's drugs everywhere and there's anti-social behaviour everywhere ... at least if we stay here, chances are if someone was to sell my kids drugs chances are when I went and knocked on that door I was going to know that person who sold it to 'em ... so I know what I'm up against and I know what sort of response I'm going to get and I know how I need to deal with it ... If I move away I ain't got a clue and I could be going up against anyone couldn't I? (interviewee 27, 7.11.05)

Those who do not have a long history on the estates, either personally, or through their families, tended unsurprisingly to be much more ambivalent about ideas of 'community'. One woman, who may loosely be described as a middle-class incomer, initially made good links with her neighbours. However, she found herself ostracized when she was, falsely, accused by a neighbour of being a paedophile:

that summer like the neighbour, our immediate neighbours, these are the next neighbours, didn't speak to us. The other side that we'd looked after their dog every summer, you know for two weeks they wouldn't speak to us and it was just horrendous, like, people that had known us for yonks, you know, really sort of got into the malicious erm, and it was horrible and if [my child] went out in the back garden they'd be abusing him from two doors down and shouting things at him and we didn't have any money but I got my overdraft extended and I in the end got a fence put up, a big fence put up which I don't like and haven't liked it ever since. It feels a bit like the Berlin Wall ... I've just wanted to move. (interviewee 43, 12.12.2005)

There are relatively few visible minorities living in the estates.[3] Three of our interviews with white longer-term residents revealed deep suspicion, and in two cases hostility, towards black people and towards Muslims. Categories such as 'black', Muslim and asylum-seeker were used by these interviewees interchangeably. Others we spoke with took a diametrically opposite position, including a young woman with a black boyfriend. One white woman and one of the few black long-term residents explained their revulsion at racist attacks by a small group of white teenagers first on a family of East Asian origin and then on a group of Fijian soldiers who had been renting a house on the Larkman estate.

A Filipino national told us that she was very happy to have moved to the estate as she now had a bigger house and was nearer to her workplace at the hospital than in her previous rented accommodation in the city. However, she and her colleague, another resident, did not feel any sense of 'community'. Indeed they told us they had not yet got to know anybody else living on the estate, except for another Filipina. Walking out to the bus stop to go to work and returning in the evening they had experienced taunts from white boys who regularly hung around in their street. To protect themselves from this on future journeys to and from work, they removed their coats to reveal their nurses' uniforms, which made them feel safe because they engendered value and respect. A resident of South Asian origin who had recently moved onto the estate spoke of his loneliness. Since moving to the estate over six months ago, no-one had invited him or his family into their house. When this happened for the first time just a week before we re-interviewed him in February, 'it was really good ... [she is] the first one who takes this kind of initiative. It was fantastic ... somebody calls you, like specially [that they are] the white people' (interviewee 29, 9.02.2006).

The Estates and Shifting Boundaries

For those who have a long link with the estates, the boundaries of their individual notions of what makes up 'their' estate are played out on a micro-scale. Far from being homogeneous, the three estates have distinct identities, which in part reflects their separate built histories – part of the North Earlham estate was built in 1927–8, before major slum clearance began in the city, and initially housed what might be seen as the 'respectable working class'. The second phase of building, in 1936–9, saw the completion of this estate and the construction of the Larkman estate, mainly to house people who had been moved out of the slum areas of central Norwich. Part of the Marlpit estate was constructed at this time, but the bulk of it was completed in the 1960s. Significantly, the busy Dereham Road runs through the area, dividing the Marlpit from the other two estates.

However, the estate boundaries are in no way clear-cut. Passengers returning from the city and getting down from a bus at the Dereham Road/Larkman Lane crossing may be heading for any of the three estates, including some relatively wealthy areas of owner-occupied housing which happen to fall within the administrative boundaries of the NDC area.[4] Yet other bus passengers, and the conductor, will name the stop as 'Larkman', which, as far as the rest of the city is concerned, carries a particular stigma and has a dangerous reputation. A community worker, now also a resident of the NELM area, said when she first started working in the area she was told by a colleague that 'at one point in its history about 60 percent of the crime in Norfolk could be traced back to the Larkman estate' (interviewee 47, 9.01.06). Sometimes people thought of as living in the Larkman (though in fact it applies to residents of any of the three estates) have been labelled 'monkeys' by other Norwich residents. For example, one of us travelling on a bus overheard a group of young people from City College talking of a fellow student and Larkman resident as being rather stupid: 'He's a monkey, monkey, monkey!' The term has been adopted by actual Larkman residents and incorporated as a motif within the mural of the local community centre – as 'Monkey Island'.

Within the three estates, however, residents create boundaries, both to do with physical space, such as the names of the particular roads included in the Larkman, say, as opposed to North Earlham, and to do with an imagined cultural world. For example, there is a tendency to shift the boundary between North Earlham and Larkman depending on whether an attempt is being made to portray the area as more respectable, in which case it is North Earlham, or less, when it becomes the Larkman. The Marlpit is commonly seen as 'posher' than the other estates – as one interviewee from the Larkman/North Earlham side of Dereham Road put it, 'they spell fuck with a capital F over there'.

> *We [on the Marlpit] don't cause trouble. All we do is just stand, sometimes have a drink, just sometimes a little bit loud. On that side of the [Dereham] road, they just go around nicking, mugging old people.* (interviewee 48, 12.1.2006)

Within the Marlpit itself are further subdivisions, as the image of respectability tends to be associated with the area of older building, while the newer area, particularly the flats, is often linked with drug dealing. In January 2006 this part of the Marlpit estate was the subject of an Anti-Social Behaviour Order, limiting the size of gatherings on the street. One respondent, an activist who had worked in the area for many years in the 1980s and 1990s, referred to the fragmentation of estate identities:

> *some people certainly on the, on the Larkman side of the Dereham Road would not see the Marlpit as being part of [the area], and the Marlpit vice versa would not see themselves as part of the Larkman ... and the Larkman was divided into ... the Monkey Island end and, and there was around the sort of Clarkson Road, Motum Road side of Cadge Road and there was the other side of Cadge Road and they saw themselves differently so Beverly Road, Ranworth etc saw themselves differently ... and I think that people didn't want to be particularly identified with Motum Road. They wanted to say, 'well, we're better' ... It's interesting how again if you have a very, a community that is, is very erm, protective of itself perhaps but it doesn't have experience of the outside world, [it] becomes very inward looking and the more inward looking you become the more fragmented that community can become and it, it sort of asserts its identity in smaller and smaller areas.* (interviewee 31, 21.11.2005)

In spite of the labels applied by (some) residents of each estate to those of the others, there is significant movement between them. For example, people commonly move between the Marlpit and the other estates, or vice versa, and have friends and family on either side of the Dereham Road. Yet, in many ways the road acts as a barrier, with people being unwilling, for example, to attend a community centre for events, as they perceive it as being outside 'their' area. Similarly, there is, what has been to us, a surprising lack of knowledge about the basic geography of estates other than an interviewee's own: in the course of a conversation, on several occasions, we have mentioned a street on the North Earlham estate, and found a life-long resident of the Marlpit not to know where it is, even though it is only 10 minutes walk away. In one extreme case, a woman who lived at one end of Motum Road where her father, one sister, mother, brother and son also all lived, described how she had panic attacks when she went beyond a certain point further up the road. Her family, embodied in that particular section of the street, represented the boundaries of her particular 'community'.

Histories of Migration

It is important to emphasize that, alongside these very individual-based micro-constructions of what constitutes the local, residents, far from being isolated, conduct social relations enmeshed in networks that commonly encompass not simply national, but transnational, spaces. This can be seen through links both into and out of the area via the migration of individuals, ideas and capital. While Norwich, and in fact Norfolk, is typically seen as having been bypassed by post-1945 waves of immigration and settlement, in fact the estates have both contributed to, and experienced, various forms of migration.

Central to the experiences of interviewees growing up during and after the second world war was the presence of American soldiers in and around Norwich. Young women from the estates met them in the city, at the bases where dances were organized, or when they visited houses on the estates. Sisters of several interviewees, in what appear to be disproportionately large numbers, married GIs and moved to the United States. Similarly, interviews, backed up in part by council minutes, suggest that significant numbers from the estates took advantage of government-assisted migration schemes to Australia in particular, commonly referred to as 'the £10 ticket'.[5] Subsequent correspondence, often supplemented by visits, has created for the family members who remained resident on the estates not only international social contacts, but also a means of being able to directly compare their life experiences with people of a similar background who made different life choices. It has also created a cohort of people who have become conversant with foreign cities, landscapes and the ins and outs of international travel.

Again, for older interviewees the armed forces, either serving in them or as a spouse, provided the means to travel the world, and to gain perspectives of life outside of 'the Larkman'. The frequency with which people from the estate lived abroad for temporary periods was vividly illustrated by one interviewee who described how, one day, she swam out to a rocky island in a bay in Cyprus. As she lay resting there she was recognized by a friend of her brother's, who lived three streets away. The result for some has been to create distance between themselves and other residents, often those of a younger generation, who are not seen as having the same breadth or depth of experiences.

> *I went through the Suez Canal on a troop ship … I sneaked up on deck didn't I, and I stood there oh, I suppose, half the night … I found it absolutely fascinating and we were in one part of it and er, there was the old Bedouin, we were in with the sheep and they were running along the side on the sand banks - oh the smell huh! But, you know, how many people have seen that? I was absolutely fascinated and when I saw the film of Lawrence of Arabia … I thought, 'I've been there, done that' … I've had a hard life and an exciting life erm, but … when I used to come home on a visit I used to think 'oh god', you know what I mean, 'oh for Christ sake'.* (interviewee 2, 9.11.2005)

For younger generations, rather than travel abroad, the primary route for leaving the area has been through the medium of education, which, again, can lead to feelings of alienation from their place of origin, as well as the ability to reflect on the costs as well as the benefits of coming from a close-knit working-class estate:

> *BR: And what would you say, you said the good thing about that, knowing where one belonged, what would you say was the bad thing about that?*
>
> *I1: Erm, was that it made, I think engendered a, for me certainly a sense of pointlessness in trying to do anything different or… that I think we're very actively knocked down or told that we were getting too big for our boots or that we were trying to do things that we were being ridiculous if we tried to do something that didn't fit into what the family expected and I know for example when I went to university one of my aunts actually didn't speak to me for several years because who did I think I was you know and er, there, there, I think it really, it really is the crabs in a bucket thing like you don't need a lid they're just, I think that's quite depressing to live amongst that I think.* (interviewee 28, 14.11.2005)

For others, being good at school was something to be avoided, not so much because of the disparaging attitudes of teachers but more because of the disadvantages anticipated if credibility was lost with peers:[6]

> *you didn't want to be a goody goody did yer, you know, that's the last thing you want teachers like you … I did enjoy sciences, I didn't want anyone to know I actually enjoy that … I can remember one year when I come top in science and they all start copping the piss and I said, 'that's alright I knew the answers', I said, 'I see the answer sheet'.* (interviewee 15, 4.10.2005)

This interviewee, and other men in their 60s and older, described the decision to join the military as the only socially acceptable way of gaining formal educational qualifications without losing face.

The temporary movement of estate residents out of the country to jobs abroad with the military led to encounters as migrants which not only left deep impressions of other people and places but which has in the process contributed to ideas about 'race' and national identity:

You might imagine on a troop ship all those people, so I used to get up early in the morning for a shave while the water's about ... I forget how many mile out [of Mumbai], 'Phew, what's that smell?'. Now all of a sudden I was talking to this here [sailor], and he say, 'you give it a half an hour you'll see what, I shan't tell you', he said, 'you'll see'. And you started to see the sea change colour, dirty old brown colour and the smell get stronger, cos you're not used to it. See once you've been there you don't notice it but er, when you get there and what they used to say ... 'jewel of the empire'! I'd never seen nothing like it in my life. First thing you see is the old bullocks walking about cos they, they let them walk about don't they, and these poor beggars with rickets walking about backwards like crabs, just ignoring 'em, never seen nothing like it. (interviewee 8, 2.11.2005)

The NELM area, over its history, has not simply acted as a source of labour for export and armed forces recruits, it has also attracted and absorbed people and ideas from newcomers with varied class backgrounds. Some of these have brought in ideas and influenced social action on the estates. This is not to suggest that all social and voluntary action on the estates has received impetus from 'outsiders' – indeed, it has become very clear to us that over the decades there has been a considerable number of voluntary initiatives emerging purely from the grassroots actions of residents. These have included the building of a church, the construction of community centres, and the formation of a patrol to protect a local school from vandalism.

However, it is equally apparent that far from being cut off from external influences, social experiences and action on the estates have been influenced by 'outsiders'. For example, the University of East Anglia was built in the 1960s, close to the NELM area. While most residents do not see it as a place they can aspire to attend, not only did residents work on the construction of the campus in the 1960s, but women from the estates have formed a pool of labour from which cleaners and other ancillary staff are drawn. One former cleaner talked with much affection of 'her students':

Oh but they're lovely. That's funny when I was turning that drawer out I found a letter in there from one of my girls who come from Brazil. I mean they're all my girls and boys all of them. (interviewee 12, 10.11.2005)

Another interviewee, an Indian national and academic who moved to Norwich as part of a job relocation to the then relatively new university, worked hard as a teacher in a secondary school in the area to counter what she saw as disadvantages based around class:

I always thought ... that they needed an extra handle ... I know partly because if you're black you need an extra handle and it's very like that. My sixth formers had to have something extra ... Because they were working class, they, they had, they came from so many disadvantages ... they had to have something extra so we had all sorts of things like we always arranged for English sixth-formers extra evenings when they would come for a play reading or listening to poetry or records or a talk. (interviewee 35, 3.11.2005)

Another middle-class immigrant to Norfolk, a former journalist, this time from north London, found it important to engage politically and socially on the estates, bringing a political ideology of equality and justice developed through experience bringing up children in socially mixed areas of the capital. She started working with women on the estates to promote healthy eating:

[My ideas] were a bit, yes they were foreign ... the classic example of that was when we did pasta sauce and pasta and ... this woman said 'I really liked that' erm, and I said 'Maybe you might like to try and make it at home during the week' and she said 'Huh no', she said 'if I made that he'd just throw it at me', and I said 'But if you really like it, you like it, make it for you' ... Anyway the next week she came back and I said 'So did you get a chance to make it?' and she said 'Yep I did cos I really liked it' ... Not only did he throw it at [her] but the following morning she had his mother and I think her sister and maybe even her mother, she had three of them on the doorstep saying 'Why are you giving him this ridiculous food? I mean this is horrible food, this is not food for a man' ... I was absolutely shocked. I was amazed and I realized one of the main things which is how difficult change was. (interviewee 31, 21.11.2006)

Other immigrants have brought capital to invest in businesses as well as ideas developed in the United States and India. Clergy in the Church of England, Methodist and Pentecostal churches in the area also carried ideas about social change, some of which were put into practice. One incumbent at a local church had instituted, prior to the Sunday morning service, a breakfast which was well attended by young people. Church buildings had been the subject both of vandalism and of community construction projects in the past.

Emerging Questions

The New Deal for Communities (NDC), a government policy to invest in 'community'-led partnerships in deprived neighbourhoods, makes the implicit assumption that community is a solid, bounded set of social relationships, located in one place. In this paper we have drawn on some of our research in progress with residents, staff and others involved in the Norwich NDC area to begin to illustrate the relationship between social identification and community in this particular place.

Feelings of belonging to a 'community' in the NDC area vary from being intense for some to being non-existent for others. Moreover, even for those who do feel they belong and are known in the area, identities have been constructed around (and in opposition to) micro-units of space inside the three estates. Belonging for some sits alongside exclusion of and even conflict with others. This complexity has been recognized in a major recent evaluation of NDCs nationwide. It suggests that 'community engagement' has been limited because 'residents can think NDCs are cliquey, offering "lip service" to consultation'.[7]

In this research, we problematized the notion of community by deliberately seeking out newly arrived residents and people who had moved away, rather than focusing only on those whose connections to the estate stretch back more than a generation. This has inevitably led to an appreciation of the huge diversity of backgrounds of estate residents, in terms of class, ethnicity and nationality. The categories ('Travellers', Irish, former rural workers and ex-slum-dwellers) that we started out with have been shown to be inadequate. Feelings of belonging to the area and being connected to other residents are highly contingent and may be related more to length of residence, family history, skin colour, nationality and relations with neighbours than history of settlement. Most significantly, echoing Doreen Massey, identity, a sense of place and a sense of group belonging may be strongly related to an individual's own migration history and their interactions with 'outsiders' bringing their own histories to the estates.

In attempting to understand the interrelationship between individual identity practices and the discourses of the Welfare State, the next stage of our research, analysis of interview transcripts and further interviews and ethnographic work, needs to build in a systematic investigation of the flows of people and ideas into and out of the area. We also need to consider why some residents have never moved, even for a break on the Norfolk coast. It is by following these pathways that we will be able to assess the actual, perhaps unintended consequences of welfare policies, including area-based initiatives, in people's lives, alongside some of their unstated intentions.

Notes

1. For details of the project see http://www.open.ac.uk/socialsciences/identities/profile_rogaly.shtml, accessed 5 April 2006.
2. http://www.neighbourhood.gov.uk/page.asp?id=617&printer=1, accessed 14 March 2006.
3. A recent report suggests that 1% of residents are 'non-white': S. Pearson, 'New Deal for Communities 2001–2005: An Interim Evaluation', *Neighbourhood Renewal Unit Research Report 17* (NDC Evaluation Consortium, 2005), November, p. 7.

4. Such as the bottom of Hellesdon Road and parts of Gypsy Lane.
5. See A. James Hammerton and Alistair Thomson's *'Ten Pound Poms': Australia's Invisible Migrants* (2005).
6. See Paul Willis's Why Working Class Kids Get Working Class Jobs (1977).
7. 'New Deal for Communities 2001–2005: An Interim Evaluation', Neighbourhood Renewal Unit (2005), November, p. 67.

Ethnicity, Identity and Community Cohesion in Prison

Coretta Phillips
London School of Economics and Political Science

'Community cohesion' is now a professed policy objective of the New Labour government. The term was coined here in the aftermath of racialized confrontations between young Pakistani/Bangladeshi and white men, amidst serious clashes with the police, in Bradford, Oldham and Burnley in Spring/Summer 2001.

These 'riots' propelled issues of ethnic identities, diversity, multiculturalism and integration to the top of the political agenda once again. Official reports into the disturbances argued the need to move beyond ethnic, religious and cultural divisions and conflict, to mutual understanding, common ground and a celebration of diversity, in order to create cohesive communities (Cantle, 2001). At its core, then, New Labour's community cohesion agenda has the expressed need for Britain's multi-ethnic and multi-faith communities to be integrated into British society through a common identity, sense of belonging, and the valuing of diversity which, it is argued, will engender shared participation in everyday life.

In its strategy on race equality and community cohesion, *Improving Opportunity, Strengthening Society*, this integrationist aim is intertwined with a reduction in social and economic inequality between ethnic groups, alongside the alleviation of social exclusion (Home Office, 2005a).[1] The relative emphasis given to these ideals in the government's discourse on community cohesion has been the subject of vehement critique, as has the proposed means of achieving them (see Alexander, 2005; Amin, 2002; Kalra, 2002; McGhee, 2003; Phillips, 2005; Webster, 2002). These issues are addressed in more detail elsewhere in this volume.

This chapter takes as its focus the nature of order and community cohesion in the prison setting, and is similarly organized around the key themes of common identity and belonging, difference and diversity, and equal participation in social life. How do ideas of 'community' and 'cohesion' translate into the prison context, and what can be learned for policy development from a study of this one social institution? This chapter draws on thinking developed as part of an ethnographic investigation of ethnicity and identity in prisons.[2]

Sociological studies of the prison have conceptualized the prison as a social system with its own cultural mores, norms, and expectations – very much like society itself. The prison has been characterized as a microcosm of society, most obviously since it draws its members from the free community (Sykes, 1958; see also Wacquant, 2001, for a more radical interpretation). At the same time, despite its physical boundaries, the prison is permeable to outside influences as many prisoners continue to have contact with their families and friends in their home communities during their incarceration. It is also the case that various forms of media, particularly in-cell television in the last decade, have penetrated the prison world (Jewkes, 2002). Thus, whilst prisons are often physically and symbolically isolated from wider society, they are deeply embedded within it.

Prisons, by and large, contain individuals who have experienced social and economic exclusion – prisoners are typically unemployed before imprisonment, are frequently without educational qualifications, and have poor numeracy and reading abilities (Social Exclusion Unit, 2002). Prisons are also ethnically diverse – in 2002, individuals from 155 countries were represented in prisons in England and Wales, and in February 2003, 12% of the male prison population and 21% of the female prison population was of foreign nationality (Home Office, 2003, 2005b). This should not obscure the consistent finding – the explanation for which has long preoccupied criminologists (see Phillips and Bowling, 2002) – that around 12% of British nationals in prison are black, which is considerably higher than their 2% representation in the general population (Home Office, 2005b). Prisons also exhibit some religious diversity, and whilst the most common faith practised in prison is Christianity, over two-thirds of Asian prisoners are Muslim (Councell, 2004). Thus, there are parallels between the prison world and some urban communities such as those in the Northern towns where racialized conflict erupted in 2001, or indeed those in the Lozells area of Birmingham in late 2005.

The potential for conflict between ethnically and religiously diverse groups within prison has similarly exercised government ministers, policy officials and prison practitioners. Current concerns have been framed by the racist murder of Asian prisoner, Zahid Mubarek, in Feltham Young Offenders Institution in March 2000. He was beaten to death by his white cellmate, Robert Stewart, who was subsequently convicted and sentenced to life imprisonment. At the time of the conviction, the Commission for Racial Equality (CRE) announced a formal investigation into Her Majesty's Prison Service, amidst broader complaints of racist bullying and discrimination in two other prisons (HMP Parc and Brixton). The CRE (2003a, b) made 17 findings of unlawful racial discrimination which cumulatively concluded that the Prison Service had failed to deliver equal protection to all prisoners in its care or to deliver race equality in its employment of staff or treatment of prisoners. Thus, the prescribed elements of a cohesive community – a common identity and sense of belonging which is inclusive of those with diverse origins, and racial equality in access to services and facilities to enable shared participation – were clearly absent from the prison communities examined by the CRE.

In this chapter, I seek to look more broadly at the issue of order and cohesion in the prison community, beginning with the question of individual and collective prison identities and socialization into prison life. Next, the role of ethnic identities in race relations in prison is examined, before reviewing the empirical evidence on racial equality within the prison world. The last section of the chapter considers the construction and negotiation of other identity positions relating to masculinity, religion/faith, age, class, sexuality, nationality, regionality and locality, and how these may contribute to our understanding of the nature of community cohesion in the prison context.

Two Models of Identity and Community in Prisons

The idea of prisoners having a common identity[3] is one that has divided sociologists of the prison. For those such as Sykes (1958) the totality of the prison experience produces a unified body of prisoners who have a functional shared identity, group cohesion and solidarity against prison staff. This 'indigenous model' draws on Goffman's (1975: 236) analysis of total institutions where, on entry, prisoners experience a painful and systematic mortification of self, resulting from a series of ritualized degradations. According to Sykes (1958) the 'pains of imprisonment' – the deprivation of liberty, goods and services, heterosexual relationships, autonomy and security – all contribute to this mortification process. The dehumanizing aspects of prison socialization have the effect of disrupting the social roles prisoners adopted outside the prison and challenging individuals' self-concepts, leading to what Foucault (1979: 236) describes as 'a recoding of existence'.

Sykes and Messinger (1960) argued that prisoners develop an 'inmate code' of values which governs social relations within the prison. The code centres on:

- loyalty towards other prisoners (*don't interfere with inmates' legitimate or illegitimate interests, don't grass/rat on another prisoner*);
- the absence of arguments between prisoners (*play it cool, do your own time*);
- the avoidance of exploitation (*don't steal from cons, don't break your word, don't be a racketeer, be right*);
- the maintenance of self (*don't weaken, be tough, be a man*); and
- a distrust of prison staff (*don't be a sucker, be sharp*).
  (see also Irwin and Cressey, 1962).

According to the indigenous model of social relations, the prison world is characterized by community cohesion and solidarity among prisoners, enforced through the inmate code which operates above any other identity positions (such as ethnicity, religion, age, sexuality, and so on), as *prisoner identity* assumes the greatest significance.

In sharp contrast, the 'importation model' emphasized the influence of external statuses and behaviour patterns on prisoner subcultures. Jacobs's (1979: 8) review, for example, regarded racial and ethnic cleavages as defining features of US prisons, subsuming the common identity of prisoner, with white and black inmates instead living in 'separate conflict-ridden social worlds' (see also Jacobs, 1977). Race and ethnicity were seen as structuring social hierarchies, the informal economy, religious activities and prisoner relations, largely through the collective opposition of Black Muslim prisoners, who contributed to the 'balkanization of prisoner society' (see also Carroll, 1974). Prisoner norms and the inmate code itself were subject to variation depending on the race of the prisoner, with white prisoners experiencing imprisonment individually or in small cliques, whilst black prisoners did not *do their own time*, but instead worked for the collective good of all black prisoners. For Jacobs, moreover, the nature of prisoner subcultures could not be divorced from the predominant presence of white prison officers governing a numerical majority of black prisoners.

Such racial and ethnic divisions have persisted in US prisons, sometimes represented through gang or religious affiliations, with high levels of self-segregation, mistrust and hostility (Diaz-Cotto, 1996; Henderson et al., 2000). It has even been argued that the new 'master status trait' (Hughes, 1971) for prisoners is racial affiliation, with no space for inmate loyalty as a generic class. Instead of prisoner solidarity against prison officers, the racialized 'street code' epitomized by 'hypermasculinist' notions of honour, respect and toughness reigns, with a blurring of the boundaries between prison and ghetto (Wacquant, 2001).

British Prisons – Parallel Lives, Parallel Worlds?[4]

Power, Ethnic Identities and Diversity

Despite a large body of empirical research in North America, few studies in the UK have examined 'race relations' *between prisoners*, instead focusing attention on relationships between *prisoners and staff*. The most comprehensive examination of race relations among prisoners was conducted over 15 years ago by Genders and Player (1989). Their research found pervasive racial prejudice among prisoners, which largely resulted in an avoidance of contact and verbal aggression rather than physical conflict (cf. Wood and Adler, 2001). Social groupings by ethnicity were noted by prisoners, but were seen as reflecting commonalities of experience rather than being conflictual (see also Grapendaal, 1990). Some evidence was found of black prisoners aggressively dominating prison facilities and activities at one institution, with 'white Gangsters' heading the social hierarchy in another prison. In the latter site, peaceful coexistence between the white elite and the less powerful black groups was the norm, although on occasion 'virtual racial warfare' erupted (Genders and Player, 1989: 103). Sometimes prisoner unity prevailed where prison staff were seen to restrict the activities of prisoners in some way. Thus, Genders and Player found support for both the importation and indigenous models. Crewe (2005a) too notes that prisons research has conclusively demonstrated the influence of both imported identities and institutional deprivations on prisoner relations, perhaps not least because the late modern British prison is not characterized by the same depth of privation that Sykes's (1958) *Society of Captives* exhibited. Physical improvements, a more liberal regime in operation by prison officers, and the introduction of the Incentives and Earned Privileges system have all contributed to the wane of the inmate code and prisoner solidarity, although it remains unclear whether this varies by ethnicity.

Prisons in England and Wales are now even more ethnically diverse than they were at the time of the Genders and Player (1989) study. This is amidst a significant increase in the overall prison population which rose 36% for white prisoners between 1985 and 2002, but 170% for minority ethnic prisoners. In February 2003, the male prison population comprised 76% white prisoners, 16% black prisoners, 3% Asian prisoners, and 5% Chinese and other minority ethnic groups. For females, the population composition was: white (69%); black (25%); Chinese/Other (5%); and Asian (1%) (Home Office, 2005b). Prisons are therefore 'mixed spaces', yet, as Amin (2002) recognizes, colour composition tells us little of the nature of interactions within that space. After all, '[h]abitual contact in itself is no guarantor of cultural exchange', possibly instead leading to established ethnic practices becoming embedded in social life (Amin, 2002: 969). Moreover, as Jacobs (1979: 23) observed, 'It is hard to imagine a setting which would be less conducive to accommodative race relations than the prison'.

Marked by mistrust, fear, high levels of verbal and physical victimization, physical and emotional deprivations, boredom, overcrowding and an intense lack of privacy, the prison setting presents particular obstacles to cohesive social relations. At the same time, unlike the lack of contact between diverse communities – seen to be a major cause of the disturbances in the northern towns in 2001 – one of the characteristic and oft deplored traits of prison life is its enforced close contact between prisoners (Goffman, 1961). Within the tense environment of the prison, then, it seems likely that ethnic, religious, national and cultural diversity could create the conditions for conflict and disorder. The empirical evidence on ethnic relations in British prisons presents a rather mixed picture.

Sparks et al.'s (1996) study at Albany and Long Lartin prisons in the early 1990s described cohesive race relations there. Exploring social order in prisons in the wake of the Strangeways siege, they concluded that ethnicity was not an organizing feature of prison life. Few black prisoners who were interviewed reported hostility or racism among prisoners, and there was the added security of a significant numerical presence of black prisoners, which provided mutual support and prevented widespread victimization. Where racial prejudice was encountered was among some older white prisoners who resented the protection given to black sexual offenders by black prisoners – an ethnicity-based allegiance similarly described by Jacobs (1979) in US prisons. This disrupted the inscribed power within the traditional prison hierarchy which is founded on notions of hegemonic masculinity (see Bosworth and Carrabine, 2001; Newton, 1994; Sim, 1994). It sets armed robbers and professional criminals at the top and 'nonces' or sexual offenders at the bottom, the latter of whom were freely victimized by other prisoners (cf. Crewe, 2005a).

More recently, a survey conducted by NACRO in 1998–9 in nine prisons found that 51% of prisoners considered relationships between prisoners of different ethnic groups to be okay, with 27% believing them to be good and 7% very good. Only 13% believed relationships to be poor or very poor, which is undoubtedly a positive finding. However, it was Asian prisoners who were more likely to report negative relationships. Victimization on the grounds of race was also found to differ quite significantly among minority ethnic groups in the recent thematic inspection *Parallel Worlds* conducted by Her Majesty's Inspectorate of Prisons (2005). Across all prison types (juvenile, young offenders, women, adult men), Asian prisoners more frequently reported racist bullying; in women's prisons, 37% claimed to have been victimized in this way. This is likely to be linked to the perception of Asian prisoners as a less powerful grouping within the prison social system, perhaps because of stereotypes regarding their physical weakness and passivity (Crewe, 2005b; Sparks et al., 1996).

Other data from prisoner surveys indicate the relationships between prisoners may be marked by racist abuse – both verbal and physical. Ellis et al. (2004), for example, reported that slightly more than one-fifth reported racist physical abuse or being bullied or threatened by other prisoners at one adult male prison and in a young offenders' institution that they studied, and one-third claimed that racist verbal abuse occurred between prisoners. In a third institution, prisoner race relations were reported to be unproblematic. In HMIP's (2005) thematic inspection, racist bullying was as or less likely to be noted by young black prisoners compared with their white counterparts, which suggests that the social dynamics of juvenile and young offender institutions are distinctively different from those of adult institutions where black men reported higher levels of victimization. In all but young offender institutions, mixed-race prisoners had lower levels of racist victimization than black prisoners. Yet in Edgar et al.'s (2003) study of victimization and conflict in seven diverse prisons, racist abuse occurred only rarely, although violence was, on occasion, sparked by cultural misunderstandings. As insults, threats and intimidation are routinely experienced in prison life, it is to be expected that some conflicts will result from tensions between ethnic groups, fuelled by racial prejudice, ignorance and racism.

Existing evidence seems, therefore, to point to relatively harmonious ethnic relations within prison, but set against a backdrop of abuse and violence, which could be motivated by racism at times in certain institutions, and more particularly targeted at Asian prisoners. This is an area where greater insight is required, particularly in relation to the construction of Asian identities, as they find themselves consistently located among the lower echelons of the prisoner hierarchy. In the light of these findings, it is significant that the Home Office's Citizenship Survey (2004) similarly reported greater racial prejudice among the general population against those of Asian origin than other ethnic groups. Understanding more about the dynamics of inter-racial (white/black, white/Asian, black/Asian) and intra-racial (particularly cross-national) conflicts within prison should also reveal more about the role of ethnic identities in contributing to order and cohesion in the prison setting.

However, it is important to acknowledge that in the NACRO (2000) survey, 87% of *prisoners* reported relationships between ethnic groups to be okay, good or very good. This compares favourably with the 59% of the British *population* surveyed by MORI who believed race relations to be good, although this rose to 67% among minority ethnic respondents (CRE, 2002). This could reflect what Crewe (2005a) found in his study of male prisoners at Wellingborough. There, prisoners reported being more tolerant and respectful of others than they would in their home communities, in part because of the deprivations and constraints imposed by the prison regime. Whether the prison environment constitutes what Amin (2002: 969) refers to as 'everyday spaces that function as sites of unnoticeable cultural questioning or trangression', and where accommodation prevails, should also be explored in future research. It is these sites, according to Amin, which offer the most promise for improved social interaction between ethnic groups.

For both policymakers and those working within prison establishments, it is also imperative that prisoner race relations receive attention in race relations policies, particularly given the provision within the Race Relations (Amendment) Act 2000, that public authorities such as prisons must promote 'good relations between persons of different racial groups'. This needs to occur alongside the important focus on the role of staff in providing equal access, services and treatment to minority ethnic prisoners,[5] as discussed next.

Racism, Inequality, and Participation

For Jacobs (1979), writing about race relations in US prisons in the 1970s, prisoner social relations had to be understood within the context of a predominantly white prison officer structure governing a majority black prison population, amidst broader societal racism. Whilst such a situation has never existed in prisons in England and Wales, it is equally true that the prison social system cannot be understood without reference to institutional controls and the racial dynamics of the way prisoners are treated by staff (but see Cheliotis and Liebling, 2006).

The historical and contemporary criminological literature on prison race relations is replete with examples of racial discrimination against minority ethnic prisoners by prison officers (see Bowling and Phillips, 2002; Phillips and Bowling, 2002). From the Genders and Player (1989) study in the mid-1980s through to the CRE's (2003b) formal investigation into the Prison Service, there is clear and consistent evidence of direct and indirect forms of racial discrimination. Genders and Player's (1989) study of five prisons, for example, found that black prisoners were stereotyped as arrogant, lazy, noisy, hostile to authority, with values incompatible with British society, and as having 'a chip on their shoulder', leading them to often be allocated the least favoured prison jobs[6] (see Chigwada-Bailey, 2003, for similar findings in women's prisons).

The CRE (2003b) investigation, conducted more than 10 years later, reported that there were failures of prison establishments to: protect against the racist abuse and harassment of staff and prisoners; remove racist graffiti; take disciplinary action against racist perpetrators; provide equally appropriate food and faith services to Muslim and black prisoners; provide equitable access to work because of the negative stereotyping of black prisoners which also resulted in their over-representation in formal disciplinary actions and drug-testing, and under-representation in the enhanced level of privileges; and to protect against the victimization of prisoners who made complaints of racism by prison officers.

Two recent studies have explored prisoners' perceptions of race relations, which are unsurprisingly more negative among minority ethnic prisoners. HMIP (2005) found that while 2% of white prisoners felt that they had been insulted or assaulted by prison officers because of their race, this increased to 17% for black prisoners, 12% for mixed-race prisoners, and 11% for Asian prisoners. It is significant that 27% of Asians in young offender institutions felt they had been racially victimized by staff, although Asian prisoners were overall more likely to feel unsafe from victimization from other prisoners (see above). Moreover, only 53% of young black prisoners in young offenders' institutions believed that most staff treated them with respect, compared with 61% of young Asian prisoners, 68% of mixed-race prisoners and 70% of young white prisoners. Minority ethnic prisoners also held more negative views about their treatment within the prison regime (in relation to categorization, work allocations, privileges, disciplinary systems, segregation and access to release schemes), and in their access to appropriate food and faith provision. These issues, exacerbated by language difficulties, may be particularly acute for foreign national prisoners (see Prison Reform Trust, 2004).

Cheliotis and Liebling's (2006) survey in 49 prisons found that minority ethnic membership (black, Asian, and Chinese/Other) was the most significant predictor of perceptions of poor race relations. Even 9% of white prisoners felt that black and Asian prisoners were treated unfairly compared to them. The proportion for minority ethnic prisoners was 42% for black prisoners, 41% for Asian prisoners and 30% for Chinese/Other prisoners. These negative beliefs were closely linked to prisoners' views about prison officers' unfair exercise of their discretion in distributing privileges, controlling discipline, providing access to information and responses to requests and applications. Their generally lower ratings on measures of dignity, trust, family contact and order have significant implications for establishing penal legitimacy among minority ethnic prisoners.

Edgar and Martin's (2004) study of four local prisons led them to conclude that processes of 'informal partiality' may operate in prison whereby prisoners come to perceive racial discrimination in their treatment by prison officers, although this cannot usually be proven. Fifty-two percent of prisoners they surveyed claimed to have been racially discriminated against but only a minority of prison officers (21%) said they had observed a colleague acting in a racially discriminatory manner. The HMIP (2005) inspection too reported that staff had vastly different understandings of racism and race relations in prison than did prisoners. According to Edgar and Martin, this disparity of perspective resulted from routine interactions where black and Asian prisoners feel they are negatively stereotyped, are more disadvantaged by prison officers' use of discretion in receiving benefits or being disciplined, and this occurs in the context of a lack of oversight or monitoring of prison officers' actions.

We have as yet no understanding of whether minority ethnic prisoners' perspectives on their treatment by staff influences their interaction with white prisoners. It is also unclear how religious identities contribute to prisoner allegiances and cohesion, but Spalek and Wilson's (2002) work has pointed to the academic and policy neglect of religious discrimination against Muslim prisoners.[7] With the increasing incarceration of Muslim prisoners for terrorist offences, this is likely to assume even greater political significance in the coming years.

Prison Identities and Community Cohesion

In drawing together the evidence on the prerequisites which contribute to community cohesion according to current government thinking – a common identity, sense of belonging, the valuing of diversity, the absence of ethnic inequalities and social exclusion – prison communities are clearly lacking many of these key elements. At the same time the empirical findings reviewed in this chapter have indicated relatively positive social relations between some ethnic groups in prison, albeit within the context of some racist victimization, abuse and discrimination, both between prisoners and between prisoners and staff. However, our knowledge in this area would be considerably enriched by a more thorough under-standing of inter-racial, intra-racial and cross-national interactions between prisoners at work, in classes, during association, on the wings and during exercise, and within different prison institutions. An insight into the circumstances in which ethnic identities are specifically articu-lated and salient (or not) in prison social relations is also required. We actually know very little about what Amin (2002: 959) refers to as 'the daily negotiation of ethnic difference ... the micropolitics of everyday social contact' in the prison setting.

An appreciation of the role of ethnicity as a resource, upon which pris-oners may draw, either to endure the pains of imprisonment, or to more directly resist institutional control, or to assist with their resettlement in their home communities post-imprisonment, is also necessary. Bosworth and Carrabine (2001) suggest, for example, that prisoners draw on their lived experiences and identities outside prison to negotiate within prison, with both other prisoners and staff. Their performances may involve mean-ingful challenges to prison authority and knowledge or be more overt in nature, but displays of power within the prison are inherently shaped by identity practices, which are themselves culturally and socio-economically constructed. Similarly, Wilson's (2003) study in a young offender institution described how young black men resisted the control imposed on them by prison 'Govs' by 'keeping quiet', occasionally 'going nuts', but above all drawing on support and solace from other black prisoners.

The complexity of men's identities within prison must also be more fully comprehended. Little is known about masculinist identities among prisoners of minority ethnic and foreign national origin, for example, and how these may cut across the traditional crime-type hierarchy within prison subcultures. The influence of black diasporic cultural forms on lan-guage, music and fashion remind us of the complex ways in which black masculine identities have been popularized and appropriated by some young white men – albeit problematically (Back, 1996; Frosh et al., 2002) whilst being actively resisted by others (CRE, 1998; Nayak, 2003), but we do not know whether this has any impact on prison social relations. It seems likely, since the use of argot in prison and the display of branded fashion remain potent signifiers of status which can command respect within prisoner society as in outside communities (Jewkes, 2002).

Crewe's (2005b: 471) work too points to the changing position of some Asian prisoners within the prison hierarchy, whose status has been (perhaps) temporarily elevated by 'powder power' and their connection to heroin sup-ply. Added to this, emerging accounts of young Asian men's assertive iden-tities in local communities, experienced through the multiple lens of religion, 'race', ethnicity, culture, class, gender, masculinity, family, age/generation, nationality and locality, also highlight the need for a more nuanced understanding of their place within prisoner subcultures (Alexander,

2000, 2005; Archer, 2001). Class-based, local, regional and national identities also feature prominently as the basis for prisoner allegiances and may at times transcend ethnic, cultural and religious identities, and thus determine the extent of cohesion within particular prisons (see Bosworth, 1999; Crewe, 2005a).

For these reasons, understanding the identity dynamics of the prison social system may enable a more grounded analysis of power relations and community cohesion, and, arguably, can suggest how community cohesion can occur in local communities where individuals are not con-strained by the loss of liberty and other pains associated with imprison-ment, but may similarly be marginalized by structural inequalities, deprivation and discrimination.[8]

Notes

1. This document appears to more equally balance the need for a common identity and sense of belonging with the eradication of social and economic inequality between ethnic groups, presumably taking on board the criticism of commentators such as Amin (2002) and McGhee (2003). However, see T. Phillips (2005) for a crit-ical analysis of New Labour's approach to reducing ethnic inequalities.
2. For details of the project see www.identities.org.uk (Research Projects – Projects) (Dr Coretta Phillips).
3. A sense of belonging to the prison community cannot, of course, apply in the same way as in external communities given that prisons are places of sufferance. As Goffman (1961) notes, inmates will frequently present a 'sad tale' or 'a line' to explain away their presence in prison; in essence, to state precisely why they *do not belong*. However, Goffman goes on to describe the colonization adaptation to prison life among some prisoners, which leads them to prefer incarceration to life outside the prison – thus belonging or 'having found a home' in the prison (Goffman, 1961: 59).
4. The term 'parallel lives' was used in the Cantle Report (2001: 9) to refer to the residential, educational, employment, cultural, religious and linguistic polariza-tion of white and Muslim communities in urban areas in Britain. 'Parallel Worlds' is the title of the recent report on race relations in prison, undertaken by Her Majesty's Inspectorate of Prisons (2005). It describes the absence of a shared understanding of race issues in prison among staff and prisoners, who appear to inhabit parallel worlds.
5. In the Action Plan on race equality developed by HM Prison Service and the CRE and the Prison Service's Race Equality Scheme, the vast majority of actions listed are concerned with services and facilities to prisoners, although one aim was to develop interventions to challenge racist attitudes and behaviour amongst prisoners (CRE, 2003a). In the current Action Plan (2005–8), there is a reference to race relations training for prisoners and the possible use of media-tion for prisoner complaints (HMIP, 2005).

6. In 1988, the Court of Appeal awarded a black prisoner £500 for being racially discriminated against. It was shown that comments based on racial stereotypes in his assessment and induction reports at Parkhurst prison had led to him being denied a kitchen job. One section of the report read: '[h]e displays the usual traits associated with people of his ethnic background, being arrogant, suspicious of staff, anti-authority, devious and possessing a very large chip on his shoulder, which he will find very difficult to remove if he carries on the way he is doing'.
7. Cheliotis and Liebling's (2006) survey reported that 62% of white prisoners and 60% of Asian prisoners felt that there was respect for all religious beliefs in prison. For black and Chinese/Other prisoners, 50% and 53% respectively felt this to be the case.
8. The study *Ethnicity, Identity and Social Relations in Prison*, represents an attempt to learn more about the social milieu of the prison in light of issues of identity [see http://www.identities.org.uk/].

8

Home, Identity and Community Cohesion

Simon Clarke, Rosie Gilmour and Steve Garner

Centre for Psycho-Social Studies, University of the West of England

The idea of community has always been central to the construction of group and individual identity. It has been the site of moral panics about the disintegration of traditional community and values as well as very real concerns around racism and segregation (see T. Phillips, 2005). The notion of community is of central importance in contemporary policy and political thinking. So, for example, as Anna Marie Smith (1992) argues in the 1980s and early 1990s, new right Thatcherite policy concentrated on creating a hegemonic project which aimed at defining social space through the construction of outsider figures. Smith argues that the construction of demonized groups, what we could call communities, allowed for a political bartering for power in which politicians claimed that the only way they could protect British families (the British family) was to have more control over local government – in other words, strengthen the authoritarian hold of central government. More recently (2006), David Miliband, as Minister for Communities and Local Government, has talked of the opposite in what he calls 'double devolution'. That is, not just devolving power to local government, but to local communities and people. Thus policy has shifted significantly over the past 20 years, but how do ordinary people feel about their sense of identity, their belonging to a community and how does this affect their lives?

In our research[1] we have set out to explore how people today construct their identities and whether traditional forms of identity construction – such as class and ethnicity – still hold. As most humans are essentially sociable creatures, much, although not all, of this identity construction takes place against the background of the communities that people live in. We have therefore looked at what people mean when they talk of a 'community', and what increases or decreases community cohesion between groups. To do this, we simply asked people to tell us about their lives and how they felt about notions of identity, home and community in their local areas. We hope that much of what we have to say reflects the views of the people we have spoken to.

Our research has focused on two major cities in the Southwest – Bristol and Plymouth – and two different electoral wards in each city. Both cities are seaports with strong seafaring traditions and long histories of immigration, transition and trading (see Clarke and Garner, 2005). A striking difference, however, is that Bristol has a history of multiculturalism and a relatively high population of minority ethnic groups, while Plymouth is very much 'white'. Over 60 respondents have been interviewed on two separate occasions, all of them 'white', as the project has focused on *their* views of identity and community, rather than those of the minority ethnic populations.

The respondents were split between the two cities and the electoral wards, and were divided evenly in terms of gender and across a spread of age groups. They were found through a variety of 'gatekeepers' such as community development workers, clergy, community leaders and youth workers. In other words, we used a 'snowball' method to obtain respondents. The sample is not intended to be representative nationally but may be indicative of ideas among the general population. We used a psychosocial perspective to inform both our methodology and analysis – a perspective that takes into account the emotional dynamics of social life and in which the researcher is seen as a co-constructor of the research environment (see Hollway and Jefferson, 2000; Clarke, 2002; Lucey et al., 2003).

The interviews from the first round of the research were biographical in nature, very unstructured and allowed the respondent to tell us what they thought was important about their life and history. In the second interviews we explored the following key themes: what it means to be British, or English, in relation to identity; the impact of this on community cohesion, in other words the difference between local and national communities; how people feel about the provision of welfare (in each case the respondent stipulated what welfare meant to them, i.e. social housing, benefits, health) in the United Kingdom. Finally, we looked at the nature of UK immigration.

Identity in Relation to What is 'Closer to Home'

Identity has been theorized at a number of levels and it is commonplace now to talk about multiple identities or cultural identity. Cultural identities are marked by a number of factors: 'race', ethnicity, gender and class to name but a few. The very real locus of these factors, however, is the notion of difference. The question of difference is emotive, and we start to hear ideas about 'us' and 'them', friend and foe, belonging and not belonging, familiarity and the unknown, in-groups and out-groups, which define 'us' in relation to other, or the Other. As Burgat notes, 'Identity is the result of the encounter with otherness' (2003: 21). A central question in this debate is who subscribes to a cultural identity and for what reason. Do we choose our identity or is it beyond our control?

From the notion of difference and the Other, we get ideas about communities, even 'imagined communities' in which all the members never get to see each other face-to-face, and ethno-national boundaries. According to Anderson:

(A)ll communities larger than primordial villages of face-to-face contact (and perhaps even these) are imagined. Communities are to be distinguished, not by their falsity/genuineness, but by the style in which they are imagined ... The nation is *limited* because even the largest of them ... has finite, if elastic boundaries, beyond which lie other nations... Finally it is imagined as a *community*, because, regardless of the actual inequality and exploitation that may prevail in each, the nation is always conceived as a deep, horizontal comradeship. Ultimately it is this fraternity that makes it possible, over the past two centuries, for so many millions of people, not so much to kill, as willingly to die for such limited imaginings. (1991: 6–7)

Anderson thus shows the strength of that community feel and of the 'comradeship' that people can potentially experience in what is, essentially, a concept, an imagining, which makes that concept something infinitely desirable and something to be striven for. Indeed, the idea of community is something very positive for people: not one of our respondents had anything negative to say about the actual idea.

Their positivity, however, was generally focused on something more localized than the nation. Very few felt that they belonged to 'the British community' and most questioned whether such a thing existed any longer. As one respondent noted, in phrases very reminiscent of Tonnies' (1988) concept of the larger-scale, more distant society (*Gesellschaft*), rather than the more familiar community (*Gemeinschaft*):

I probably wouldn't stick British and community together. They wouldn't be two words that I would attach because probably British I see it as a kind of nationwide whole country kind of governmental thing, and I probably wouldn't use community to describe something that size. So I'd use community on a smaller scale level where I think there is meaningful relationship and interaction between people. And I think on that level, I don't think British would be a term I would use to describe things on that level, even though probably the majority of people in that community would be British, or those communities would be British. It wouldn't be the thing that defines it to me.

In the same way, the vast majority of the respondents were clear that Europe also offered them nothing in terms of their identity. The tendency was invariably to focus on the smaller scale and there was a strong desire on the part of many respondents to have their Englishness rather than their Britishness recognized. There was some resentment that the other nations within the United Kingdom could and did celebrate their heritage and their individuality, but that somehow England could not and did not:

> *Q How do you feel about being British?*
> *A Quite happy about being British, but more so English. It's just one of those things. The Scots are patriotic about being Scots, the Welsh are patriotic about being Welsh, the Irish are patriotic about being Irish, and if you're patriotic about being English, there's something wrong with you. This is the sort of attitude I feel that in this country we don't stand up for it, for who we are, the distinction of being English as opposed to being British as the Scots or whatever would say they're Scots and British second, so that's where I stand on that one.*

Many stressed that they wanted to write English as their nationality or ethnic origin on forms and were annoyed that mostly they did not have this opportunity. Several identified being English as important in the sporting context, others saw it as more connected with their ethnic roots, while Britishness was applicable on a more global and a more political scale, useful in other countries and on passports:

> *British has come to mean something to do with being part of Europe, being part of a wider almost global society, and English is something you might find in country villages if we had any country villages anymore. And to do with people who are humble and rooted in this country, actually rooted in the soil, in the place.*

Others preferred their Englishness to Britishness for more negative reasons. While some were proud to be British and expressed pride in the royal family, the history, freedom of speech, democracy, others saw it as something much more negative and talked of British people behaving badly abroad and of terrorists and expressed the view that Britishness was now 'diluted':

> *British has ceased to mean something that stands for honour, courtesy, good government, integrity. It doesn't have any integrity in it any longer, so if somebody asks me what I am now I say I'm English.*

Cultural diversity was seen positively by many respondents; others, however, felt that Britain has lost or is losing at least some of its identity, with most talking about this in the context of multiculturalism and 'political correctness' with regard to old British customs such as those surrounding Christmas. Several mentioned that 'Christmas' now had to be replaced by 'winter-time' and that carols, nativity plays and Christmas decorations had been banned in several places for the sake of other cultures. While some directly blamed those other cultures for the changes in British customs, others directed their anger more towards those in power who were being overly sensitive about the needs of ethnic minorities. Many respondents, however, particularly those who were less well-off, expressed their concern about the numbers of people being allowed into the country, about Britain being seen as 'a soft touch' in relation to other countries and about the negative effect that the perceived open-door policy would have on the British population:

> I would definitely say that we're an easier country than a lot of other countries. I would say we're just too easy. We're just a country that is just being taken advantage of, and yet ... it's neglecting people that already exist in this country and they're sort of not looking at people that are British citizen, you know, people that are already here, looking at people that come to the country.

In the case of many people, their potential confidence in their larger, national identity, if they felt it existed, thus seemed seriously threatened and many seemed much more at ease with a more local identity situated in the notion of community.

Identity in the Context of Community

Returning to Anderson's notion of 'imagined communities', our respondents' imaginings were limited to what they knew and could experience first hand, despite being exposed to the concept of the larger national community through the media. There is a need to experience the reality of that community physically through such concrete manifestations as local institutions, the schools, the church and youth clubs, and there is extreme resentment when such institutions are threatened or removed. Many respondents of all ages said that community disintegrates without them, especially schools, around which so many relationships between both children and parents are built. Taking away the school takes away a sense of ownership from the community. One of our areas in Plymouth and one in Bristol have lost their secondary schools, and the other Bristol site does not have its own secondary school.

> You feel 'us against the world', that sort of attitude develops, when you attack a school, you attack its community as well.
> I can't think of anyone I've met who's had an involvement with the school in the past who's not felt a real sense of loss from it closing. And obviously especially the kids that were going there until a year or so ago, they've not got anything good to say about the change at all, but are very negative about it... The expression I keep hearing from a number of people is that it seemed to sort of rip the soul out of the area for a lot of people.

The lack of a local secondary school means that after the age of 11, the children have to attend schools elsewhere. This leads to the disintegration of school-based networks which often involve mothers. It also increases mobility and transitoriness among the local population, as families may move to get their children into the secondary school of their choice. This fosters a sense that the community cannot offer residents what they want and therefore they are willing to put less into the community.

Some take it further and view the disintegration of the networks as having far-reaching consequences, potentially leading to crime and territorial in-fighting. The 18-year-old son of a respondent in Plymouth had been recently attacked in the local park by a group of young adults slightly younger than him, and he had been shocked that he didn't know any of them, not even as the brother or sister of someone. Her other son had been threatened in the local pub which he rarely went to. The respondent thought this might have been linked to the closure of the secondary school: the children had been dispersed among different schools in other areas and had therefore not gone on to the local youth club and then on to the local pub together. In other words, social progression within a local community had been disrupted and had led to local residents not knowing one another. Parents no longer knew who the local children were and therefore couldn't keep an eye on them or keep them in check by potentially talking to their parents about them.

At both sites where the local secondary school had been closed, there was widespread resentment towards 'them' (usually identified as the local authorities) for having taken the action, and a perception that it had been done on the authorities' agenda without the consent of the local community. There was a sense of a large part of the community identity having been removed and this then having repercussions for individual identities, which then have to be reconstructed in another context. Identities therefore become 'a multi-faceted phenomenon', no longer stable but open to different influences that vary according to the context (Back, 1996: 50).

One reconstruction of such lost identity is visible in the increase of tribal or territorial tensions, 'atavistic divisions' (see Henry Tam, this volume) within both the areas that have lost their secondary schools. One respondent in Bristol described how tangible this tension was at a local youth club attended by teenagers from two adjacent residential areas in the city, how one group complained when the other group arrived from the area which had lost its secondary school and tried to provoke them by calling them names connected with their residential area. The respondent commented that going to a new school in the other area was really difficult for that group because of the territorial rivalry:

> *They went to their sworn enemies if you like. It was the same when we were at school, there was fighting amongst the schools.*

Parents in Plymouth tried to avoid such overt conflict in a similar situation. When the children who would normally have gone to the local school were offered places in a college in a neighbouring area with which our area had traditionally hostile relations, the parents preferred to have their children bussed to schools miles outside the city or attend schools further away in Plymouth. So the boundary drawn around an area can sometimes be more important than those drawn within it.

The construction of tribal identity and territorial rivalry, however, is not restricted to schoolchildren. Adults 'inter-marry' [sic] within their own residential area and thus reinforce their local identity:

You never saw, hardly ever saw foreigners here, so there was a very insular, and even if you came from, I mean, if you lived in Devonport and you moved to some parts of Plymouth, what's regarded, it's all Plymouth, but Devonports regard themselves as separate, there's rivalry there. There's rivalry between Efford and Eggbuckland, they don't intermarry. One of the things I've noted with the work I do is that families don't marry outside their estate, it's almost like they're a village, like Efford. They'll marry within Efford and ... Swilley will marry in Swilley, you don't marry from St Budeaux if you live in Swilley.
Q It's all tribal stuff.
A Very, very tribal.

Local residents acknowledge this construction of identity, so important to those involved in it, and there is again criticism of outsiders with power who do not accept such constructions and impose irrelevant and inappropriate ideas on communities, which ultimately reject them:

There's a lot of tribal relationships, I can only put it like that, in these areas, where everybody knows everybody else and is inter-married and inter-related. I think it is not only at a local level, but at a global level, people ignore these tribal structures and try and impose very, very foreign unworkable structures on them. The people who they're imposed on don't understand. They don't understand how it works. They quickly revert to what they do understand which is their tribal affinities and loyalties and so on.

Identity and Community in the Notion of Insiders and Outsiders

The construction of boundaries between insiders and outsiders throws up mixed messages. In both cities there was an acceptance of a clear distinction between insiders (generally those born and brought up in the city) and outsiders, with insiders proud to acknowledge their status, and outsiders equally keen to acknowledge they were not insiders.

In Plymouth there was a great deal of ambivalence expressed by residents about those who have chosen to stay there or who are Plymouthian:

Plymouth people are odd for the most part. If they've got any get up and go, they usually do get up and go, so the ones that are left are sort of 'drecly', a Cornish expression, like the Spanish mañana.

In Bristol there is sometimes a feeling of outsiders not being accepted by the 'genuine' Bristolians:

> *Bristolians are not given to spilling the beans about themselves. I have met loads of them over the years and I have to say that if I had my time to come over again, I might have chosen somewhere else where the natives were more open and more friendly. Most of our friends are immigrants, you know, from Wales, Scotland, London, the North wherever, because Bristolians are very cliquey, they stick together.*

The clear distinctions made between insiders and outsiders assume more subtle forms. One resident, discussing why there were few minority ethnic people, argued that no one would be against it, but questioned whether they would share the local values.

Identity and Geography within the Community

There is obviously a perception that particular places are repositories of distinct sets of values. Some are felt to be somehow more authentic repositories of local values. In both Plymouth and Bristol, the centre of the city was viewed as a site of 'real' local identity, likewise south of the river in Bristol where there used to be more industry, whereas in Plymouth the city centre is close to the waterfront and the naval base. We could thus interpret this as linking notable industry with urban identification, as industry is a key determinant in a city's make-up and in the lives of its inhabitants. One respondent in Plymouth was at pains to stress that those who lived on the outskirts of the city could not feel the same kind of local identity felt by those who lived in the centre, although this was now changing as a result of mobility and people moving out of the city centre.

Community is Identity

Some identify so strongly with their community that it becomes their identity. One couple in 'Edgefield' are so involved in building a community on their estate that they have had their living room extended so that they can hold children's craft clubs in there regularly (44 children and 6 adults at one time in their house is their record) and are admired as a potential role model by other residents:

> *Community is what you make of it... Some people bury themselves in their family life, which is great. Others are different – like Jack and Kathy [names changed]. He'd like to be like them in his 60s/70s. It's like having a second Mum and Dad really with them two.*

While such a level of involvement in the community is rare, there is general admiration for those community members who put themselves out to take an active part and an acknowledgement that it is generally women who take the lead, often in a school context. A striking finding from our work is also the extent to which community groups are kept active by the older generations:

> The problem is that 'no one is coming through the ranks as a youth who'd like to keep the community spirit going. They're all thinking of each other now instead of thinking of others, they're all ... what they can get out of life, not what they can get out for other people or what they can do for other people ... It's all one vision now, it's what can I do for me?

Yet some perceived participation in the community as a duty that benefited the individual, acting as a counterpoint to potentially 'claustrophobic' family relations, benefited the nation and led to better national behaviour.

What Attracts People to Identify with their Community?

Humans are essentially sociable creatures and community is all about people, a shared vision and shared values. These engender a sense of trust and belonging, the notion that other people are there for you and that you're not alone:

> It's just knowing your neighbours, it's having people around you, it's working with them, just working, shopping, interfacing, you just meet with them and bump into them occasionally, getting to know the people around you, that gives you a sense not just of security, but belonging, and things like that, ownership, those sort of words.
>
> I think it is having contact with people who live near you who have got similar ideas and values to you, a feeling that you're not alone, that you're not cut off, that if you had a problem, you could ring up a neighbour and they would come and help you or you could knock on someone's door and they would help you and also vice versa as well, and being able to walk down the street and talk to people. I think that is an important thing about community. It's just generally including everybody and that you do feel as if you're not in a little box and that you don't speak to anyone else around you.
>
> You can't think you belong to anything really until you do something for the community, can you?

A key element of community is also the familiarity that goes with it, not just with the people, but also with the local geography, affording a certain sense of ownership of the terrain and creating a feeling of safety. We found that the familiarity was a very comforting concept for respondents of all ages:

> *Q It sounds as if you felt you were really part of a community there.*
> *A Mmm! Just in the sense of knowing people from school because I wouldn't feel intimidated at going anywhere in my area because I knew people rather than if, you know, if you went into an area you didn't know, you would feel intimidated and you know, people's perception, you think, 'Well what are you doing here? Why are you here?' Rather than, you know, I was like, when we was at school I could go literally anywhere in my area because there was people there that I knew from school. You know what I mean? Then people wouldn't be looking at me, going well, what are you doing here? Do you know what I mean, round this area, stay away from our area. From where I was in school, I could just go anywhere.*

And yet community takes place outside the home, specifically among the working classes who appreciate being able to meet friends outside but being able to shut their doors afterwards.

Factors Detrimental to Community

Mobility in the population is clearly instrumental in the weakening of long-term social ties. People change jobs much more frequently which often means they move house and so they are often less willing to spend time and effort in what may be, for them, a temporary community. They move house as an investment – a relatively new social phenomenon; they move for their children's education. Houses are often thus seen as stepping-stones rather than something more permanent. This is a fundamental change in social relations and in how people view themselves in the context of their perhaps temporary communities, as Bauman notes, quoting Richard Sennett's *Corrosion of Character*:

> 'No long term is a principle that corrodes trust, loyalty and mutual commitment', but nowadays 'a place springs into life with the wave of a developer's wand, flourishes, and begins to decay all within a generation. Such communities are not empty of sociability or neighbourliness, but no one in them becomes a long-term witness to another person's life'; under such conditions, 'fleeting forms of association are more useful to people than long-term connections'. (Sennett in Bauman, 2001: 38)

Bauman points out that the degree to which an individual is immobile is today a measure of social deprivation, with sedentariness now viewed as a liability, whereas the mobility of those who can move because they do not have strong local commitments is one of 'the major stratifying factors on the global as much as on the local scale'.

Our respondents were also aware of movement across boundaries. Whilst some people we spoke to had lived in the same city all their lives, others had travelled, lived and worked in different parts of the UK and abroad. The reasons for this might have to do with a career path (their own or their parents'), with attending university, with marriage, or with forced movement due to evacuation in wartime, which we found among older people in Plymouth particularly. Mobility was much more marked among the more middle-class respondents, while those on the estates often tended to stay there for years, if not all their lives, and, even when they had moved away, they often moved back. Some were aware of the potential stigma this might bring, particularly where property is concerned:

> *But there is that underlying thing that if you live on a council estate, you have a particular social standing and if you have moved out of a council estate onto a private property and own your own property which isn't ex-council, then you're somehow slightly superior.*

Changing work patterns have also contributed to a loss of traditional community spirit: people work very long hours and come home with little desire to go out again. This also contributes to the lack of interest from younger people in community matters: they do not necessarily have the time and/or the energy quite apart from the motivation. Quite a few expressed the view that they would probably participate in their local community later on in life.

The effect of cars was also singled out as detrimental to community building. People get straight into their cars to go off to work and so don't have the opportunity to talk to their neighbours. Driveways were also seen as adverse, providing a divisive space and a barrier to communication, whereas in the old-style terraced houses people had much more opportunity to talk to their neighbours. One Bristol resident described the car as

> *... a wonderful thing as a personal convenience but it isolates people in another way. I mean, you know, 30 years ago or 50 years ago, nobody had motorcars and everybody shopped, and I think the community was much stronger then than it is now.*

Here one of the consequences of modern life is identified as having a particularly negative effect, worsening living conditions and insulating people from close contact.

Consumerism and materialism were also identified, particularly by older respondents, as detrimental factors in the building of community spirit. Many respondents were at pains to stress that when they were younger, they were happy with what they had or were given and knew not to ask for more, whereas several commented that children seemed to expect more and more material goods, regardless of the cost, and that they were generally given far too much these days.

> *As you get more of the things in life, it seems there's less caring for other people. People seem to close their door, and they don't want to know others, they want their barriers like.*

One Bristol resident, close to retirement age, noted that it was very difficult to persuade younger people to come out to functions such as barn dances; they tended to be more interested in staying at home with a video and a take-away. Several of the female respondents also commented that families were more and more likely to eat in front of the TV, not communicating with one another, all eating at different times, often microwave dinners.

Identity, Community and the 'Golden Age' Discourse – Nostalgia and Loss

Les Back (1996) describes an estate in London called Riverview which had been designed in the 1960s 'as a showcase of post-war reconstruction', and which had subsequently been seen for about a decade as an aspirational estate to move to. This was viewed as the 'golden age of community' when the local population was established and stable, they were the 'estate people', there was no crime on the estate, everyone knew one another and children could safely play all over the place. Then there was a new policy of allocation, and 'problem families' were moved in, many of them less well-off and from minority backgrounds. This created hostility among the established families towards the newcomers, a hostility which was accompanied by a nostalgia and a yearning for the stability and predictability of the Golden Age.

At one of our Plymouth sites, many of the problems on the estate were attributed to 'problem families', and, in both Plymouth and Bristol, to tearaway children and teenagers whose parents didn't bother about them. Problems such as drugs, burglaries, stolen vehicles and harassment were usually attributed to the problem families and the children. These problems were generally identified as relatively new, and there was a nostalgia for earlier periods in the history of the community when such issues apparently did not arise:

> *You could go just anywhere when I was small and not worry about it but you wouldn't let kids do it nowadays because of what is happening now, you know.*

> *Looking back, it was nice because everybody was always there for you, but you never felt they lived in your houses.*

Many of the more elderly respondents remembered with affection and a sense of loss the times when nobody locked their doors, when the milkman would just walk into the house to collect his money from the table, even if nobody was there, and when nobody got burgled or had their property stolen. They remembered a time of much greater neighbourliness, particularly those who could remember the war years, when people really 'looked out' for their neighbours. There were expressions of nostalgia for the loss of such community spirit, which had involved collective trips, looking after each other's children and the time to develop intimate relationships.

There is an active movement to recreate a traditional community at one of our Plymouth sites, where a range of activities, including welcome packs for new residents, the provision of classes for adults and for children, and the institution of a local festival have been driven by a couple who explicitly acknowledge that they are seeking to recreate something like what they experienced as young people. Similarly, at one of the Bristol sites, a local society is striving to maintain a focus on community, rather than individual, activities, holding events in the Village Hall, negotiating as a group with the Council for the benefit of the community, and promoting the re-introduction of traditional elements such as a weekly Farmers' Market.

There is quite clearly no one 'Golden Age' narrative that we can accept on face value, with each generation expressing nostalgia for different ideas and forming strong senses of identification with different lifestyles. So, while this type of nostalgia may form the basis of community cohesion and solidarity we also have to be aware that strong attachments to community have a Janus face. Strong identification with certain ways of life often brings with it exclusionary practices, the definition of who we are by the denigration of others, and ultimately racism (see Clarke, 2003). Some time ago Martin Barker (1981) identified what he called 'new racism' based in culture and 'ways of life' which emphasizes difference between cultural communities rather than inferiority. This creates emotional attachments that lead to both fear and ambivalence for other groups, communities and cultures.

Anna Marie Smith (1992) has also highlighted the way in which outsider figures have been used in political projects to define the boundaries of social space and therefore communities. Smith's work was an attempt to reveal the new right hegemonic project of the 1980s, which proclaimed itself the only alternative to central government policy chaos and the disintegration of the 'British' family – a far cry from Miliband's 'double devolution'.

In a more tangential but we feel tangibly theoretical way, Zizek (1993) has argued that the bond that holds a given community together is the way in which we share our enjoyment. What we fear most is the theft of that enjoyment by others. Our enjoyment is made up of all kinds of things, ways of life, mythologies. It is the way in which we imagine our community to be and therefore is often based in a nostalgic attraction to another way of life that never really existed or has been lost. This has been exemplified in several studies (Seabrook, 1973; Rustin, 1991; Hoggett, 1992). Rustin (1991) highlights Seabrook's work in Blackburn in the 1960s, whereby the Asian community started to take on some of the characteristics of the white working class while simultaneously, through economic decline and disintegration, the white working class suffered a loss of these qualities. The white community projected into the Asian community the demoralized and disintegrated state they were experiencing in the form of hostility towards the Asian community. Similarly, Paul Hoggett's (1992) study of Tower Hamlets shows that tension between communities corresponds to a period of sustained uncertainty for groups and individuals where both group and collective identity is challenged and undermined. Often one community takes on the lost characteristics of the other. Indeed, for Hoggett, the resentment between white and Bangladeshi communities is 'made poignant by the fact that the latter community has many characteristics – extended and extensive kinship networks, a respect for tradition and male superiority, a capacity for entrepreneurship and social advancement – which the white working class in the area have lost' (Hoggett, 1992: 354).

We feel therefore it is important to ask what community cohesion actually means, what it is, and consider the detrimental, as well as the positive aspects of a strong community attachment. Because all our respondents are 'white' these views very much reflect the construction of 'whiteness' in contemporary Britain, but they also highlight that 'white' is very much a bucket category and therefore we prefer to think in terms of Stuart Hall's (1992) idea of 'new ethnicities', i.e. that we all speak from a particular place, history and experience. White identities are very much constructed from multiple experiences, geographical locations, community and attachments and multiple ethnicities.

Conclusions

This is not an exhaustive list of the ways in which people have talked about identity and community. But it does give some very general ideas about how people feel they create and maintain their identities and how this process relates to notions of community. Many of the ideas are based in what we might call 'tradition' and an emotional attachment to certain ways of life, to intimate relations rather than instrumental ones.

Moreover, there was very little talk of what we might term fluid postmodern consuming selves, narratives in which the individual is sovereign and the community is of little importance. Rather there was an emphasis on the family, class and geographical locations, which was in turn linked to ideas about outsiders and defining your self by who you are not. Interestingly there was a strong emphasis on the notion of a shared identity that linked in with the notion of community. There was also a deeply psycho-social element where people have often created their perceptions of others in their own imagination, which helps them create who *they* are. This was exemplified in the discussions of what it is to be 'Bristolian' or 'Plymouthian', where we started to see the emotional dynamics involved in notions of contempt, acceptance and tribalism between geographical areas and groups of people. Identity or identities in contemporary Britain are certainly complex and often contradictory. Community is often expressed as a feeling or something concrete such as a building. When you look at the notion of identity and community together then there is a very strong sense of boundary, both physically and psychologically. We have ideas of belonging and not belonging, a sense of who we are in relation to Others, of in-groups and outgroups and of shared values and ideas. Finally, there is also the notion of familiarity and a certain yearning to return to more traditional forms of community, albeit that those forms of community are often imaginary and unreal.

Note

1 For details of the project see www.identities.org.uk (Research Projects – Projects) (Dr S. Clarke).

9

Prejudice, Intergroup Contact and Identity: Do Neighbourhoods Matter?

Miles Hewstone, Nicole Tausch
University of Oxford

and

Joanne Hughes, Ed Cairns
University of Ulster

Living Together, Living Apart

If newspaper headlines can be believed, members of different ethnic, racial and religious groups still live largely separate lives in contemporary Britain and Northern Ireland: 'Four out of 10 whites do not want black neighbour, poll shows' (*The Guardian*, 19 January 2004); '90% of whites have few or no black friends' (*The Guardian*, 19 July 2004). But what are the implications of living together, or living apart? In this contribution we explore different, pessimistic and optimistic, perspectives on mixing and consider what the available data tell us.[1] We then present some data from our own recent research in Northern Ireland, which evaluates the impact of merely sharing a neighbourhood with members of other communities as opposed to engaging in real face-to-face contact with them. Finally, more speculatively, we consider the possible consequences of mixed neighbourhoods for social capital, emergent social identities and social cohesion.

Mixed Neighbourhoods: Threat or Opportunity?

There is a considerable body of research relating ethnic prejudice to the percentage of ethnic minorities living in a defined area. Unfortunately, the results of this research are mixed (for a recent review, see Wagner et al.,

2006). Most studies show that as the percentage of ethnic minorities increases, so do prejudice and discrimination in the majority group (e.g. Taylor, 1998). Other studies show prejudice reducing in response to a certain percentage of minorities, but then increasing again. In one of the more recent studies, Forman (2003) used data from a nationwide sample of senior pupils at American high schools. He reported that an increasing percentage of black students in a school was associated with less white prejudice, but that if the percentage of black pupils exceeded 35%, then attitudes became more prejudiced.

As Wagner and colleagues (2006) point out, these mixed results reflect competing theoretical positions concerning the relationship between ethnic composition and prejudice. On the one hand, 'threat theory' proposes that an increasing number of ethnic minority members will threaten the majority's position (Blalock, 1967) and that prejudice is a response to this perceived competition (LeVine and Campbell, 1972). On the other hand, 'contact theory' contends that an increase in the number of ethnic minority members will increase the opportunity for positive intergroup contact, and there is plentiful evidence that increased contact is associated with reduced prejudice and improved intergroup relations (see Pettigrew and Tropp, 2006; Brown and Hewstone, 2005). Using data from a national sample in Germany, Wagner et al. found that prejudice decreased as the percentage of ethnic minorities increased; this finding was due to increased opportunities for positive contact with minority group members. Having outgroup friends is especially effective in challenging prejudice. Phinney and colleagues (1997) found that ethnic diversity outside schools in the United States was associated with more cross-group interactions inside the school and more positive attitudes. Also in the US, Hallinan and Teixeira (1987) reported that the more black students there were in a classroom, the more likely a white student was to choose a black peer as a best friend.

We propose that it is not a simple matter of sharing a space – whether residential, occupational or educational – with outgroup members. What matters is whether any meaningful cross-group contact ensues. Where it does, we expect outgroup proportions to be associated with less prejudice; where, however, there is simply co-presence of two or more communities, and especially where the proportion of outgroup members is high, we expect outgroup proportions to be associated with increased prejudice.

Segregation and Intergroup Contact in Northern Ireland

Catholic and Protestant Communities Set Apart

A crucial characteristic of Northern Irish society that helps explain many aspects of the long-term conflict is the extreme degree to which its two principal religious communities are segregated (see Hewstone et al., 2005).

Even though segregation is not the cause of intergroup conflict, it plays a key role in establishing and maintaining conflict between communities. A major, but by no means the only, type of segregation between Catholics and Protestants is residential (e.g. Poole and Doherty, 1996). As Boal, Murray and Poole (1976) pointed out, the functions of segregation include provision of a base for self-defence, avoidance of embarrassing contacts with unfriendly outsiders, preservation of a way of life, and a base from which to attack enemies. There is, in short, safety in segregation, and residential segregation increased as a direct result of large population movements in response to intimidation, as families moved from religiously mixed areas into safe havens dominated by their co-religionists.

This segregation sustains conflict by creating a social climate that fosters mutual ignorance and suspicion (Gallagher, 1995). However, unlike some other apparently intractable conflicts, the potential for contact between members of the two communities in Northern Ireland exists in many areas (Cairns and Darby, 1998; Trew, 1986). For example, in the cities, even where working-class housing areas in particular are more highly segregated, people often travel out of their own area to work, thus increasing the potential for contact in the workplace. There are also residential areas of mixed housing.

The 'Contact Hypothesis'

Notwithstanding extensive segregation and a history of intergroup conflict Catholics and Protestants do come into contact with each other, but previous research agrees that much of the contact is superficially courteous, and not of a degree to alter suspicions or change stereotypes (see Niens, Cairns and Hewstone, 2003; Trew, 1986). In its simplest form, the 'contact hypothesis' (Allport, 1954) proposes that bringing together individuals from opposing groups 'under optimal conditions' (Pettigrew and Tropp, 2006) can reduce prejudice and improve intergroup relations. Allport (1954) suggested these positive effects were most likely if three main conditions were met. First, there should be equal status among the groups who meet, or at least among the individuals drawn from different groups, who meet. Second, the situation in which intergroup contact occurs should require cooperation between groups towards a common goal. Last, the contact situation should be legitimized through institutional support. Our extensive program of research in Northern Ireland is consistent with Allport's (1954) view, whether using representative samples of the adult population of Northern Ireland or students at the desegregated University of Ulster.

In one study we used data from a representative sample of the population of Northern Ireland, to investigate the impact on prejudice of two different kinds of measures, and thus explore the competing predictions concerning group composition: threat vs contact (for more detail, see

Hewstone et al., in press). The first type of measure was the mere *number* of outgroup neighbours; the second measure was actual, self-reported *contact* (we included measures of contact with outgroup neighbours, outgroup contact at work, and contact with outgroup friends). We tested whether any or all of these measures predicted outgroup attitudes (measured with a reliable five-item scale). We hypothesized that they could do so via one or both of two routes. The first route was *direct*, the predictor would simply be directly associated with outgroup attitudes. The second route was *indirect*: the predictor would affect intergroup anxiety which, in turn, would be associated with outgroup attitudes. Stephan and Stephan (1985) define intergroup anxiety as the anxiety felt at the prospect of experiencing contact with the outgroup, compared with the ingroup. They propose that intergroup anxiety stems mainly from the anticipation of negative consequences for oneself during contact, and its major antecedents include minimal previous contact with the outgroup. Intergroup anxiety has been identified as a major mediator of the effect of contact on prejudice: positive outgroup contact reduces prejudice via decreased intergroup anxiety (see Pettigrew and Tropp, 2006).

The pattern of relationships between the variables was equivalent for subsamples of Catholic and Protestant respondents, so we tested a model based on all respondents. The model revealed the impact of cross-group contact. All three measures of contact were positively related to outgroup attitudes. Contact at work and, especially, outgroup friends had direct, positive effects on outgroup attitudes, and both contact with neighbours and number of friends had indirect effects via reduced intergroup anxiety. But the mere *number* of outgroup neighbours was negatively associated with outgroup evaluation; *more* outgroup neighbours were associated with *less positive* outgroup attitudes. This is consistent with earlier analyses, suggesting that outgroup proportions can constitute a threat (e.g. Taylor, 1998).

To summarize, these findings point to a clear difference in the impact of mere number of outgroup neighbours and actual contact with those neighbours. As expected, forms of friendship contact are the most potent predictors of outgroup attitudes, and they have their effects via reduced intergroup anxiety. Contact with outgroup neighbours can contribute to improved intergroup relations, but the number of outgroup neighbours tends to be associated with worse outgroup attitudes. Overall these data suggest that the presence of outgroup members in a neighbourhood can have contradictory effects. If outgroup members are present in relatively large numbers, but without this opportunity for contact being taken up, then this variable is likely to function as a proxy for threat (see Wagner et al., 2006). Where, however, the presence of outgroup members leads to more actual intergroup contact, and that contact is positive (e.g. cross-group friendships), then its effects will be positive, promoting more positive outgroup attitudes.

Indirect or Extended Contact

Having demonstrated the effectiveness of direct contact, our research program has also shown the effectiveness of so-called indirect or extended contact. Wright and colleagues proposed that a similar beneficial effect might also stem from 'vicarious' experiences of friendship, that is, from the knowledge that other ingroup members have outgroup friends (Wright et al., 1997). They provided both correlational and experimental evidence in support of this hypothesis. They also argued that indirect friendship might have even greater potential for achieving harmonious intergroup relations than direct friendship, because it is easier to implement than direct friendship and can improve intergroup relations without every group member having to have intergroup friends themselves.

We confirmed the indirect cross-group friendship hypothesis in Northern Ireland, in two surveys (the first on a sample of Catholic and Protestant students at the University of Ulster, and the second on a representative sample of the population of Northern Ireland; see Paolini, Hewstone, Cairns and Voci, 2004). In subsequent research we have also shown that whereas cross-group friendships rely, to a certain extent, on opportunity for contact (e.g. living in a mixed neighbourhood, or attending a mixed school), this is not true for extended contact.

We believe that the relatively new idea of indirect or extended contact may be an important one in any society as strictly segregated as Northern Ireland. Extended contact may impact on intergroup relations on a wider scale than its absolute numbers would suggest, via a 'ripple' effect (one person's outgroup friends also affecting the attitudes of others who are not direct friends of the outgroup member). We are currently undertaking new work which explores the impact of indirect and direct forms of contact in residential areas undergoing transition from segregated to mixed communities.

Generalization of Contact Effects across Outgroups

Thus far, we have focused on how direct and indirect contact with members of a specific group can bring about changes in the way people perceive and evaluate that 'target group' and its members. We have recently explored another consequence of cross-group contact, namely generalization of positive effects from a target outgroup to other outgroups. In a detailed survey of over 3800 majority group respondents in four European countries Pettigrew (1997) asked respondents both their attitudes towards large minority groups in their country and whether they had friends of another nationality, race, culture, religion or social class. In all samples, Europeans with outgroup friends scored significantly lower on prejudice measures. Those with intergroup friends were also more liberal about immigration policy; they were more likely to believe that the presence of immigrants was good for their country's future, that immigrants' rights should be extended, that all immigrants should be allowed to stay in the host country, and that naturalization should be made easier. Moreover, friendship was associated with reduced prejudice towards nine different minority groups, showing that the positive effects of friendship with one group can generalize even to groups not directly involved in the contact.

We followed up this idea in a second survey in Northern Ireland. We investigated whether Catholic and Protestant respondents' experience of cross-community contact (i.e. Catholics with Protestants, and vice versa) would generalize and promote reduced prejudice towards ethnic minorities in Northern Ireland (Hewstone, Hughes and Kenworthy, 2006). This is a significant issue in Northern Ireland, given a sharp increase in racially motivated attacks, linked to Loyalist paramilitaries (see *The Guardian*, 30 May 2006). As expected, respondents reported quite low levels of contact with ethnic minorities, significantly lower than levels of cross-community contact (the official ethnic minority population of Northern Ireland is only 14,000, although it is probably closer to 35,000, but it is still a tiny proportion of the population of 1.67 million, of which 43.76% are Catholics and 53.13% are Protestants). However, an index of cross-community contact (the quantity of such contact multiplied by its quality) predicted attitudes to the religious outgroup which, in turn, predicted attitudes to ethnic minorities. Thus those respondents who had high-quality contact with the religious outgroup were more positive towards this group, and were also more positive towards ethnic minority outgroups. Hence diversity can have spin-offs beyond the initial target outgroup with whose members respondents have most experience.

Social Capital, Emergent Social Identity and Social Cohesion

Segregation and Social Capital

Social capital theory (e.g. Putnam, 2000) holds that social networks have value, being a resource for individuals and vital to the creation of a meaningful modern community. Social capital refers to connections among individuals – social networks, norms of reciprocity and trustworthiness. However, social capital does not only have positive manifestations (e.g. mutual support, cooperation, trust); it also has negative ones (sectarianism, own-group favouritism, corruption). The challenge for diverse societies is to maximize the former (but between, rather than within communities) and minimize the latter. Thus Putnam refers to 'bridging' and 'bonding' forms of social capital, respectively. Bridging social capital is inclusive and can generate broader identities and reciprocity; the 'weak ties' that link *between* networks (Granovetter, 1973) are, in fact, extraordinarily strong and important precisely because they link networks and promote social cohesion. Bonding social capital, in contrast, is exclusive, inward-looking and tends to reinforce exclusive identities and homogeneous groups. By creating strong ingroup loyalty, it may also create outgroup antagonism. Clearly we need to build bridging social capital in ethnically heterogeneous neighbourhoods, yet some research on conflict and diversity suggests that bonding social capital may be lower in heterogeneous (more diverse) than homogeneous areas (see Blokland, 2003; Vasta, 2000). Our research already suggests the importance of face-to-face contact, not mere coexistence, for building tolerance.

We have some initial data, again from Northern Ireland, that speak to these issues. As Postmes and Branscombe (2002) have shown, the impact of environmental composition (segregation vs integration) on various indices (e.g. economic deprivation, health status and psychological well-being) is complex (see also Reidpath, 2003). Notably, there is mixed evidence on segregation and social cohesion; for specific groups, segregation may foster feelings of group acceptance, but it may also promote feelings that one is rejected by the outgroup. We followed up some of these issues using the Young Northern Ireland Life-and-Times Surveys over three years (2003, 2004, 2005). We were especially interested in comparing Catholic and Protestant 16-year-olds living in mainly ingroup, mixed, and mainly outgroup areas (Tausch, Hewstone and Cairns, 2006). We found that living in mixed areas was associated with having more outgroup friends, and less ingroup bias, and that these young people viewed their neighbourhoods just as positively (e.g. 'friendly', 'people look after each other', 'feel safe at day-time') as did respondents living in mainly ingroup areas.

Segregation and Identity

An unexplored feature of diverse networks, thus far, is emergent forms of identity. It is a well-established fact that the potential for intergroup conflict may be reduced in societies that are more complex and differentiated along multiple dimensions that are not perfectly correlated, rather than being split along one central, typically ethnic or religious, fault-line (see Crisp and Hewstone, 1999). These societal arrangements reduce the intensity of the individual's dependence on any particular ingroup for meeting psychological needs for inclusion or 'belonging' (see Brewer, 1993); this, in turn, reduces the potential for polarizing loyalties along any single group distinction and perhaps increases tolerance for outgroups in general. There is also extensive empirical support for the view that people do have multiple group identities (see e.g. Deaux, 1996, for a review), and in our future research we plan to study emergent forms of identity as areas within traditionally segregated cities undergo demographic transformation. We will also study the effect on outgroup attitudes of holding multiple social identities.

An important issue is whether social identity consists of one, strong identity (made up of superimposed identities), or whether identities are multiple and cross-cutting. Brewer and Campbell (1976) used the term 'converging' categorization to label the situation in which others can be classified as outgroup members on multiple dimensions; it is a situation in which discrimination is likely to be increased. Many instances of inter-group conflict in the real world involve just such multiple converging social categorizations. For example, in Belfast, Northern Ireland, Catholics and Protestants tend to live in different places (e.g. Ardoyne vs the Shankhill Road), espouse different politics (Nationalist-Republican vs Unionist-Loyalist) and even support different football teams (e.g. Cliftonville vs Linfield). Unfortunately, in Northern Ireland, as often in situations of intergroup conflict where one basis of social categorization is dominant, there are few social categories cross-cutting the religious dimension (Cairns and Mercer, 1984).

An alternative strategy to cross-cutting identities is to try to replace existing identities with a new, superordinate common ingroup identity. The common ingroup identity model of recategorization seeks to alter *which* categorizations are used and to replace subordinate ('us' and 'them') with superordinate ('we') categorizations (Gaertner and Dovidio, 2000). There is extensive experimental support for the common ingroup model (there is also support from survey research, but here the evidence is generally weaker). Overall this research finds, as predicted, that bias is reduced primarily by improving attitudes towards former outgroup members, due to their recategorization from outgroup to ingroup.

There are, however, two major limitations to this solution (Brewer and Gaertner, 2001). First, a common ingroup identity may only be short-lived, or unrealistic, in the face of powerful ethnic and racial categoriza-tions. Second, for groups with a history of antagonism, and for minorities who are likely to resist assimilation into a superordinate category that is dominated by a majority outgroup, the prospect of a superordinate group identity may constitute a threat, which actually increases bias. Perhaps the fundamental limitation of the recategorization model, however, is that it threatens to deprive individuals of *valued* social identities in smaller, less inclusive groups. By eradicating or replacing original categorizations, this model is unlikely to meet the dual needs of both belonging to ('assim-ilation') but also being distinct from ('differentiation') other groups (see Brewer, 1993); it is also unlikely to provide cognitive simplicity and uncer-tainty reduction, two potential benefits of categorization. Thus recatego-rization is a temporally unstable solution to the problem of intergroup discrimination (Brewer and Gaertner, 2001).

But how realistic is such a model in a context such as Nothern Ireland? Again using data from the Young Northern Ireland Life-and-Times Survey (2003–5) we investigated how many Catholic and Protestant 16-year-olds living in mainly ingroup, mixed, and mainly outgroup areas adopted exclusive religious identities ('British' for Protestants and 'Irish' for Catholics) or a more inclusive, common ingroup identity ('Northern Irish'). Great interest has been expressed in recent years in the possibility that an increased number of Northern Ireland's citizens might endorse this inclusive identity (e.g. Cassidy and Trew, 1998). We found that, over-all, somewhat more respondents adopted a Northern Irish identity in mixed than segregated areas (30.6% vs 23%). However, this difference was found only for Catholics: almost twice as many Catholics adopted this identity in mixed than segregated areas (25.3% vs 13.4%). The proportion of Protestants adopting this identity was almost identical in both types of area (37%).

When we compared those respondents with an 'ingroup' religious identity (i.e. either Protestant or Catholic) with those who adopted a superordinate 'Northern Irish' identity, we found that the latter subgroup showed reliably less ingroup bias. Using more sophisticated analyses we then developed a two-step model to predict bias in favour of the religious ingroup. First, neighbourhood opportunity for outgroup contacts, together with school opportunity for outgroup contacts and participation in cross-community projects predicted contact with outgroup friends and adoption of an inclusive superordinate rather than an exclusive ingroup identity. Second, both contact with outgroup friends and adoption of a more superordinate identity were negatively associated with bias. In the absence of longitudinal data, we cannot, of course, say whether more tolerant, inclusive people live in mixed areas, or whether they develop in this way as a result of the experience. We hope to resolve this issue with future, longitudinal research.

Gaertner and Dovidio (2000) subsequently developed the dual identity model, which recognizes that groups should not be made to forsake their identities. This hybrid model simultaneously recognizes both different and common group memberships, and is a more complex form of super-ordinate identity than a simple one-group representation (i.e. the common ingroup identity model). The dual identity model aims to reduce bias by allowing subgroups to maintain their original and distinctive identities while also sharing a common superordinate identity (Gaertner and Dovidio, 2000). Because the subgroups are both members of the same group at a superordinate level, bringing them together should not arouse motivations to achieve distinctiveness, increase perceived threat to identity, or exacerbate bias. Research has found that a dual identity led to more positive outgroup attitudes than did a superordinate identity alone, especially if the superordinate category was too inclusive and did not afford adequate distinctiveness (see Hewstone, Turner, Kenworthy and Crisp, 2006).

Social Identity Complexity

A dual identity may be thought of as being a more complex form of identity, involving as it does two related identities. Roccas and Brewer

(2002) proposed that individuals' representations of their multiple group memberships can vary along a dimension they call *complexity*. Social identity complexity refers to an individual's subjective representation of the interrelationships among his or her multiple group identities. It refers to the degree of overlap perceived to exist between groups of which a person is simultaneously a member. If someone's cognitive representation of their social identities is low in complexity, this indicates that they perceive a high overlap between both the typical characteristics of their various social category memberships, as well as an overlap between the actual members of those same categories. In other words, low complexity is a high overlap between membership and characteristics. High complexity, by contrast, is the opposite. It implies that the representation of each ingroup category is distinct from the others, both in characteristics as well as membership. Roccas and Brewer showed that low complexity is associated with lower outgroup tolerance, less openness, and greater intergroup bias. More recently, Brewer and Pierce (2005) reported that higher levels of social identity complexity (more cross-cutting category memberships) were again associated with greater outgroup tolerance, but also with greater support for affirmative action and multiculturalism. Greater complexity was also related to higher education levels, liberal political ideology and age.

Numerous related research questions for the future emerge from this integration of research areas. In mixed areas do traditionally dominant categories such as race, ethnicity and religion become accepted as merely one of several cross-cutting identities? What is the relationship between social change and social identity complexity? What is the relationship between the complexity of social identification and the complexity of the social environment in which it occurs? Does perceived threat lead to simplified representations of both ingroups and outgroups? What are the links between processes of social identification and the development of social capital? Do individuals with strong ingroup identification necessarily have strong social bonds? Can social bridges be established without weakening bonding ties?

Conclusions

In this short contribution we have tried to show some of the implications of living in more diverse, and less segregated, social environments. At risk of being labelled 'Panglossian' we tend to adopt an optimistic, rather than pessimistic, perspective on mixing. We see the benefits of diversity in terms of offering opportunities for contact, but we do not deny that in some circumstances it poses perceived threats to economic livelihood, identity and traditional ways of life. Our own data from Northern Ireland support this positive interpretation and show the benefits of engaging in real face-to-face contact with outgroups, and adopting more inclusive identities, and the possibilities for building social capital in heterogeneous neighbourhoods. Many questions await future research, through the theoretical exploration of concepts such as social capital, emergent social identities, and social cohesion in mixed and segregated neighbourhoods.

Note

1. This chapter was funded, in part, by a research grant from the Economic & Social Research Council (RES-148-25-0045) 'Social identity and tolerance in mixed and segregated areas of Northern Ireland' as part of its 'Identities and Social Action' Research programme.

PART III

REFLECTIONS AND THE WAY AHEAD: TOWARDS NEW DIALOGUES

Authors reflect on points raised in Parts I and II and respond to them, generating some new thinking about the way ahead.

10

Cohesive Identities: The Distance between Meaning and Understanding

Claire Alexander
London School of Economics and Political Science

Identity Nurtured and Dismantled

In 2000, the Runnymede Commission on *The Future of Multi-Ethnic Britain* published 'a vision for Britain' as a 'community of communities' – a place 'in which all citizens are treated with rigorous and uncompromising equality and social justice, but in which cultural diversity is cherished and celebrated' (CFMEB, 2000: 15). Six years on, the ground has shifted subtly, but decidedly, in political and policy terms away from this pluralist vision of Britain as a multicultural mosaic, and in favour of a reinvigorated and assimilative national project captured in the notion of 'community cohesion'. David Blunkett, as Home Secretary, has insisted on the promulgation of 'shared norms and values', citizenship tests and oaths of allegiance, and commentators from both right and left have pronounced and embraced 'the death of multiculturalism' (Kundnani, 2002; Goodhart, 2004) – albeit for very different reasons. Even the Chair of the Commission for Racial Equality, Trevor Phillips, has pronounced that '"multiculturalism suggests separateness" and added that the UK should strive towards a more homogeneous culture with "common values ... the common currency of the English language, honouring the culture of these islands, like Shakespeare and Dickens"' (*The Observer*, 4/4/04), and has recently admonished British Muslims 'We have one set of laws ... and that's the end of the story. If you want to have laws decided in another way, you have to live somewhere else' (*The Guardian*, 27/2/06). Phillips's stern put-up-or-leave policy is a stark but telling indicator of the demand for integration that lies at the heart of the government's policies on community cohesion, in which citizenship – the right to belong and be accepted as British – has become increasingly contingent on the adherence to 'norms of acceptability' (Blunkett in *The Telegraph* 10/12/2001). 'Community cohesion' then should be understood as defined through an implicit series of oppositions masquerading as choices and riven with moral valencies – Britishness (good) versus multiculturalism (bad), cohesion (good) versus diversity (bad), citizenship (good) versus community (mainly bad), majority (good) versus minority (bad), 'us' (good) versus 'them' (very bad and probably dangerous).

Of course, beyond the recognition of the formal dimensions of Britishness as legal status or nationality, there is little agreement on what British citizenship might actually entail, what its civic, social and political responsibilities are or, crucially, what 'acceptable' cultural norms and values it encapsulates. What is it, then, to be British? Is it Gordon Brown's three principles of liberty, responsibility and fairness (Faulkner, 2006), Blunkett's English language facility, Phillips's evocation of Shakespeare and Dickens, John Major's village spinsters on bikes, cricket on the green and warm beer, Norman Tebbit's cricket test? Can it be acquired by new arrivals who know how to find the local post office, can use a phone box and are prepared to swear allegiance to 'the United Kingdom ... its values, rights and freedoms', as the new citizenship test suggests, or, as David Goodhart has controversially argued, *pace* Enoch Powell, is it a product of birth and (extremely selective and narrowly focused) history 'something we do not choose but are born into... a shared history, shared experiences and, often, shared suffering' (2004). As David Faulkner has noted (2006), there is an unresolved tension between a forward looking, inclusive version of Britishness and a (more dominant) backward looking, exclusive and nostalgic Imperial nationalism, which denies diversity, either historically or contemporarily, and maps too easily on racialized notions of belonging or alien-ness.

While there is nothing new about these debates – indeed, as the Parekh Report itself persuasively argued in 2000, historically 'Britishness ... has systematic, largely unspoken racial connotations ... Race is deeply entwined with political culture and with the idea of nation' (CFMEB, 2000: 38)[1] – this (re)turn to discourses of integration and nationhood marks a dramatic shift away from the public and political lip-service paid to ideals of multiculturalism and 'celebrating cultural diversity' of the past two decades towards one which simultaneously marks out minority communities and cultures as an obstacle (or threat) to a viable modern national identity and demands their submission and dissolution within it. It is important, then, to be aware of the contemporary moment – its continuities and dissonances – in which the government's policies on 'community cohesion' take shape. This demands a recognition not only of the recent events which have shifted popular and political discourse towards ideas of nationhood, citizenship and solidarity, but also of the longer history of postwar migration and 'race relations' in which 'community cohesion' can be seen as merely the latest attempt to '*manage* (or contain) diversity'.

It is, I think, significant that the community cohesion agenda arises in (a typically knee-jerk response) to civil unrest – in this case the 'riots' in the northern English mill towns in 2001 – as earlier policies had in the 1980s (and the fear of unrest before that – for example, around the 1976 Race Relations Act). There is some irony in the fact that while in the 1980s the response to the unrest was multiculturalism, by 2001 it was these same multicultural policies that were seen as the problem rather than the solution (Kundnani, 2002). In the 1980s the problem was seen as the lack of a strong cultural identity, to be developed and nurtured through multicultural projects; in 2001, the problem was identified as an overdeveloped sense of cultural identity, which was to be dismantled and dissolved into a common citizenship. What the policies share, however, is an emphasis on social control rather than social justice, and the focus on the cultural inadequacies of minority ethnic groups rather than the need for wider social reform.

Of course, the discussion about community cohesion differs in significant ways from its predecessors. Where in the 1980s the communities most under scrutiny were Britain's African-Caribbean settlers, the main targets for community cohesion are Muslim (predominantly South Asian) groups. The privileging of religion as a primary marker of racial/ethnic difference is a key shift and one which, in the wake of the 11 September 2001 attacks in New York and the subsequent War on Terror, has placed issues of (in)security and terror at the heart of state responses to new and established minority communities, and seen the rolling back of humanitarian obligations around asylum and the commitment to civil liberties. The tension between global geopolitics and national and local conflicts is also new, particularly with the moral panics around 'homegrown terrorism' after the events of 7 July 2005.

However, the continuities are important – it is still racialized young men who are the emblem of social disorder and the focus for punitive forms of social control, just as it is women who are the targets of social and cultural reform (black single mothers in the 1980s and subcontinental brides in 2001), and community patriarchs/'representatives' who are required to provide easy, off-the-peg 'cultural' solutions (Kundnani, 2002). Declarations of social justice are still offset by the stronger call for containment and punishment internally and immigration control externally (Alexander, 2005; Allen, 2003; McGhee, 2005), minority communities are still an 'alien wedge', within but not of the nation (Gilroy, 1987), and it is minorities themselves who are still positioned as 'the problem'. 'Identity' is still wielded as both the problem underpinning ethnic inequality and its solution, and 'community' remains the sticking plaster for society's ills. Racism remains conceptualized as primarily the outcome of individual prejudice and ignorance, segregation is proclaimed as a matter of choice and both can be seemingly overcome by bussing schoolchildren, reading Shakespeare and holding inter-faith events.

In many ways, then, community cohesion is a familiar strategy – one which harkens back to the early attempts to assimilate ethnic minorities into mainstream culture through the Community Relations Councils of the 1950s (so maybe Trevor Phillips is merely taking the CRE back to its roots). While subsequent multicultural policies, despite their many faults, at least suggested the possibility of mutual exchange, the integrationist tactics of contemporary community cohesion offer instead access to Britishness, the mere possession of which will somehow magically resolve issues of inequality, racism and exclusion. The cultural traffic, however, is strictly one-way – minority into majority – while recent state moves around immigration and asylum, crime and security, religious hatred and freedom of speech ensure that the goal remains aspirational rather than attainable. Meanwhile the Home Office pays lip-service to the notion of cultural diversity within national unity, but with a clear message that difference is only acceptable within strict limitations – i.e., to para-phrase Stuart Hall, a difference that really makes no difference (2000).

Clearly, on one level, the new community cohesion agenda stands as a monument to the inadequacies of these earlier approaches and seems des-tined to repeat their mistakes (as tragedy, or farce?) by reinscribing essen-tialized notions of race, ethnicity and culture as the source of dissent and inequality. The 2001 'riots' are undoubtedly a bleak testament to the fail-ures of four decades of 'equal opportunities' and 'race relations' policies, but what is less clear is whether these failures are down to a lack of Britishness, as is claimed, or the failures of Britishness in truly insisting on the inclusion and equality of all members of its imagined nation. Ash Amin (2002) has convincingly argued, for example, that the 2001 unrest should be understood less as the result of lives lived separately (but cer-tainly not equally) than as a demand for full inclusion into the national project – as Britishness unfulfilled.

There is an unresolved tension at the heart of 'community cohesion', then, between the assertion of a common citizenship/nationhood, the position of diverse ethnic, racial and faith communities and the ongoing issues of social, political and cultural marginalization of minorities, both as collectivities and as individuals. As Bhikhu Parekh comments:

> What values and loyalties must be shared by communities and individuals in One Nation ... How is a balance to be struck between the need to treat people equally, the need to treat people differently, and the need to maintain shared values and social cohesion? (CFMEB, 2000: xv)

These tensions have been explored in the chapters in this book, which uniquely brings together academics, policymakers and practitioners work-ing with issues of ethnicity, identity and equality, and which examines some of the possibilities and limitations of 'community cohesion' as an idea(l) and a strategy. Both individually and as a collection, the chapters present a wealth of telling and provocative insights into these issues. While I am unable to cover all of these there are, I think, three main, interlocking, themes that emerge across and between the papers, that are worth revisiting here, albeit briefly.

Three Emerging Themes

The Tension between Equality and Diversity

In 1966, Roy Jenkins famously asserted that the aim of Britain's race relations policies was to promote 'Integration… not as a flattening process of assimilation but as equal opportunity, accompanied by cultural diversity, in an atmosphere of mutual tolerance' (Solomos, 2003). Forty years on, the sentiments are well-worn and (over)familiar, although the balance between integration, diversity and tolerance has perhaps rather shifted (McGhee, 2005). At the same time, as the latest Home Office publication on 'Improving Opportunity, Strengthening Society' (2005a) acknowledges, equality for many minority ethnic communities remains out of reach in most spheres of life. In the wake of the 2001 'riots', community cohesion was severely criticized by many academics and policymakers as overlooking these issues of structural disadvantage in favour of a more palatable UK version of the 'culture of poverty' (Amin, 2002; Alexander, 2004; McGhee, 2005) – of promoting the idea of 'parallel lives' over issues of racism, discrimination, racial violence and social (rather than cultural) marginalization.

The chapters by Henry Tam of the DCLG and Nick Johnson of the CRE both address this tension, and in strikingly similar ways. Both agree that 'integration' or 'community cohesion' cannot be achieved or demanded without the move towards equality of opportunity and life experience; both acknowledge that this goal is far from being realized, and both assert that 'communities' are pulling further apart and becoming polarized. They argue for the urgent need for action to redress ethnic disadvantage and inequality, and offer structural solutions. For Tam, the solution is what he terms 'progressive solidarity', which ensures the full participation of all groups in civic and political life so they can develop 'the confidence and abilities to come together with each other and with public institutions in shaping the decisions which affect the destiny of their country, their fellow citizens and their own communities'. This cannot happen, he asserts, where there is wide disparity in wealth distribution. Johnson similarly argues that integration depends upon three factors: equality, participation and interaction. For Johnson, equality is 'an absolute precondition for integration' and demands what he terms 'thick' equality – the removal of all structural barriers to success so that achievement is based on individual merit alone 'his or her talent, ambition or desire'. Participation, as with Tam, is about giving 'all communities a voice' (though presumably the 'participation' of the 2001 rioters isn't part of this 'voice'). Interaction is predicated on the idea of Britain's supposedly increasing social and cultural segregation – that 'communities in Britain live with their own kind… [each] hardening in its separateness' – and echo Trevor Phillips's concerns with the emergence of a US-style ghettoization.

Rhetoric aside, both authors are less clear about how these aims are to be achieved, outside of the policies that have been tried, retried and have failed for the past four decades. For me, one fundamental question arises around the seemingly causal links between social and spatial segregation, cultural identity and poverty. Johnson's piece, in particular, repeats the Ouseley/Cantle/Denham truism that segregation arises (a) from choice/cultural preference, that this (b) leads to cultural separation, which perpetuates values in opposition to mainstream cultural values, and (c) this somehow, in and of itself, creates conditions of poverty and exclusion. The emphasis, then, remains on *culture* rather than *structure*, on internal rather than external factors, as the primary driver of exclusion and alienation, and thereby places the demand for change on ethnic minorities rather than broader society. Most of all, it places the responsibility for social change on individuals and communities rather than the state – a move which has seen the disappearance of 'institutional racism' from the agenda almost completely (see Coretta Phillips's chapter).

Both Tam and Johnson argue that the embracing of a shared cultural identity will promote the mutual recognition and support necessary for a reinvigorated local and national 'community' identity that lies at the heart of 'the good society'. Interestingly, Tam points to Scandinavian countries as the epitome of this national/community identity, balancing the recognition of the public realm against the uncertainties of the deregulated global marketplace. The question remains, however, as to who gets included in the national/community 'us' and who remains excluded – it is worth reflecting, for example, that those same Scandinavian societies are struggling with the realities of increasing ethnic diversity and, certainly in Denmark and Norway, this has led to the proliferation of Far Right extremist groups and anti-immigrant policies at the heart of government. 'Progressive solidarity' in action?

The Meaning of 'Community'

At the heart of the community cohesion project, of course, lies the idea(l) of community, in which Blunkett's shared norms and values provide an overarching identity lived through at the level of the individual citizen, the local and the national (but not the global – diasporic communities are significantly absent). 'Community' is valorized as encapsulating the mutual respect, support and equality that characterize a cohesive society, although its boundaries are rather more ambiguous. At times, 'community' is coterminous with Anderson's 'imagined community' of the nation, at others it seems to refer to local spaces, at others to the network of connections that form the basis of social and cultural capital; for some, such as Goodhart (2004), it is a synonym for ethnic homogeneity founded in kith and kin. 'Community' can be positively or negatively valued – the basis for Tam's 'progressive solidarity' or for Johnson's segregated/ multicultural dystopia. Ethnic minorities are usually held to have the *wrong* kind of 'community', the wrong kinds of values and the wrong kinds of connections; although, ironically, as Goodhart has remarked, they are sometimes attributed precisely the elements of cohesion, mutual support and 'thick solidarity' that are the object of government desire and national aspiration (but here negatively valued). And, of course, 'community' can be inclusive or exclusive, so that even within local spaces, it is riven by gender, racial, ethnic, religious or class divisions, and the nation itself can be a source of local conflict – what Les Back (1996) has termed 'neighbourhood nationalisms'.

As Benedict Anderson has argued (1983), all communities are 'imagined', and this makes them at once an impossibly shifting foundation for government strategy and tantalizingly open to the possibilities of reimagination. A number of the chapters in this collection explore the complex and changing contours of 'community', as it is lived and experienced at the level of the empirical and the everyday. The chapters by Ben Rogaly and Becky Taylor on 'Monkey Island' and by Simon Clarke, Steve Garner and Rosie Gilmore on Bristol and Plymouth both illustrate the complex ways in which individuals imagine and live community, so that 'the local' is reinscribed not only through geographical space, but through networks of family and friends and histories that define who belongs to the community, and who does not. Too often, it seems, those who do not belong are marked by ethnicity/race – an attitude which belies the premise of minority 'self-segregation' on which 'community cohesion' is based. As Clarke et al. remind us, the boundaries of 'community' are predicated as much by difference as sameness (see Brah's chapter), and the discourses of Britishness, belonging and cultural values are used to exclude rather than include 'Others'. Both these new studies additionally argue that 'community identity' is constructed through external structural factors, government policies and institutional neglect – that 'community' is not a pre-existing and benign natural alliance, but is constructed as much by the state as individuals. It is interesting, and telling, that both of these papers are focused on 'white' communities, and that the explanations proffered focus more on class than cultural marginality, on neglect rather than deviance, on social exclusion rather than cultural segregation from the mainstream – something which gets too often lost in the work on minority ethnic communities. White communities, it seems, are easily positioned outside of the remit for cultural reform implicit in the community cohesion agenda (see Johnson's paper for a critique of this) and ongoing processes of white flight – segregation by choice, surely? (Amin, 2002) – are seen as natural and unproblematic.

Coretta Phillips's chapter on 'Ethnicity, Identity and Community Cohesion' similarly explores the tension between the external construction of community and its internal dynamics of sameness and difference in the enforced cohesion of the prison. She argues that prisons can be seen as microcosms of wider societal processes – while on the one hand the prison setting *imposes* shared norms, values and cultures, it also *imports* broader social attitudes and divisions, particularly around race/ethnicity, gender and sexuality (versions of shared hyper-masculinity), which provide limitations on the possibilities and forms of social interaction. Drawing insightful comparisons between the world of the prison and British society, Phillips argues that 'community' is constructed and lived in multiple ways, creating 'relatively harmonious ethnic relations ... set against a backdrop of abuse and violence'. She points particularly to the differential positioning of diverse ethnic minorities within prison life – most notably the exclusion of Asian (mainly Muslim) prisoners – which raises important questions around the notion of equal participation and choice, even within this very constrained social setting.

What each of these chapters also points to is the tension between 'community' as an abstract idea(l) and a more individualistic and fluid construction centred on personal networks (what I have elsewhere termed 'personal communities' [2007]). Nevertheless, the chapters also point to the strong affective, emotive dimension of these community identities; that individuals locate themselves as part of groups – neighbourhood, estate, ethnicity, religion, class, family, friends – and that these establish enduring bonds of solidarity that cannot easily be overcome, nor perhaps should be (see Brah's chapter). As Dilwar Hussain argues in his chapter, it is important for communities to be able to develop themselves as well as engage in dialogue with other communities on terms of equality and respect. It is these relationships that form the solid core of community allegiances and constitute both the possibilities and limitations of community cohesion.

Understanding Identity

The third theme, which underpins all the papers and the themes discussed above, is around how we think of identity, and in particular how we conceptualize the relationship between the individual, the group or 'community' (whatever this may be) and the nation. As Rob Berkeley has argued (2006), the dominant discourse around community cohesion has shifted away from Britain as a 'community of communities' towards Britain as a 'community of citizens' in which it is the rights and responsibilities linking an individual to the state that are always paramount.

However, as argued above, people often locate themselves in relation to more immediate and more tangible sets of ties and obligations that stand between, and mediate, the state–citizen relationship. Conversely, the role of citizen can also mediate, or conflict with, the ties to family and community. How we understand identity, then, becomes crucial to how we understand community, ethnicity and diversity, how policy is formulated and the boundaries of citizen and nation drawn.

While identity can be viewed as internal, personality-led and psychologically driven, it has long been recognized that this individualistic approach has to be located within broader societal constructions and limitations – for example, around social categorizations of race/ethnicity, gender, class, sexuality and so on, as well as within social groupings, whether nations, 'communities' or families. Identity is formulated and experienced at the intersection of these internal and the external factors. Academic narratives of identity have increasingly moved towards the assertion of open, shifting and increasingly multiple forms of identification – of identity defined by choice, lifestyle and performance – but it can be argued that in political rhetoric and policy practice, identity remains much more simple, neatly bounded and static. This is certainly true in the discourse surrounding community cohesion, in which ethnic (particularly minority) identities are transfixed either side of the cultural barricades – parallel rather than hybrid or even multiple lives. Ethnic minorities – and particularly Muslims – are positioned as homogeneous, bound by culture and tradition and defined through lack. This is despite the wealth of academic empirical and theoretical work – my own included (2000) – that has illustrated the complex and contested forms of identity construction within and across these groups. Dilwar Hussain thus points to the ways in which current debates around Muslims in Britain overlook the internally diverse and multiple identities of these individuals and communities. Hussain's paper is crucial because, of course, it is 'the Muslim community' which is the primary target of community cohesion discourses and practices. His chapter locates Muslim identities at the intersection of local and global, political and private, issues and concerns, and explores some of the ways in which cohesion can be addressed 'on the ground'. The positioning of Muslims in community cohesion discourses raises difficult questions about how such identities/ communities get represented, and by whom, as well as how such representations are reflected, or refracted, in policy and politics. The rise of extremisms of all kinds points to the dangers of the deployment of absolutist notions of identity and antagonism – and the success of the BNP in May 2006's local elections dramatically illustrates how seamlessly these absolutisms mesh with current debates about Britishness and belonging.

Some of these contours and pitfalls of identity theory are traced in Avtar Brah's chapter on 'Non-binarized Identities of Similarity and Difference'. Brah is a leading scholar of identity theory and her work has long been engaged with putting academic theory into political practice, and in challenging essentialist constructions of racial and ethnic identities. Her chapter explores the tensions between ideas of the individual versus community, the importance of difference and its relationship to cohesion (what she terms 'affinity rather than antagonism'), and the difficulties of translating academic insights into policy. She notes, importantly, that ideas of identity and difference take shape within institutional regimes of power and political practice and argues for the recognition of context – put simply, that 'difference' is not only constructed, but is *made to mean* within specific historical and cultural setting. She implicitly raises the question of what forms of difference are being put into play in the reinvigorated discussions of nation and citizenship, and crucially, why now and here? More importantly, she asks how difference can be revalued and utilized as a basis for affinity rather than antagonism – 'how do we help create socio-economic and political conditions that are conducive to the fostering of caring and empathetic subjectivities?'

Concluding Comments

Two questions remain fundamental to the question of identity, ethnic diversity and community cohesion: what kind of society do we want to live in, and how might this actually be achieved? An additional implicit question might be, what (or perhaps, whom) are we willing to sacrifice in the pursuit of this 'good society'? Writing this a few days after the raid on a 'chemical weapons factory' (masquerading as a family home) in Forest Gate (June 2006), I have in mind the chilling comments from Tony Blair that the extreme force and the shooting were acceptable in the face of the (as it turned out, imagined) threat to the greater good. I doubt Abdul Kahar would agree or, indeed, Jean Charles de Menezes. It is hard, I think, to take seriously the professed commitment to diversity and equality, and the possibility of a cohesive society, when minorities are not only subjected to ongoing unequal, and increasingly explicitly coercive, treatment by the state, but asked to collude in it, to accept it and even to see it as justifiable. It is hard to buy into Britishness when the rhetoric of nationhood closes its borders against you, when the language of equality and social justice is used to proclaim 'rights for whites' and when the electoral success of Far Right groups is seen not as something to be challenged, but to be bartered for by ministerial carpetbaggers. For me, the chance of England winning the World Cup – along with the millions of St George crosses fluttering from car windows – didn't stack up against these odds: though I realize I may have been in a minority (again) here.

One of the biggest ironies of the 'community cohesion' agenda is that it creates the idea of minority ethnic communities at the same time as it demands their disappearance, and that it fixes ethnic identity within these community boundaries while demanding it move outside of them (Alexander, 2004). Of course, in reality, people do not live inside these neatly bounded categories, and the notion of 'community cohesion' cannot contain the multiple identities, messy encounters and human exchanges that characterize everyday life and 'convivial cultures' (Gilroy, 2004) in a stubbornly multicultural nation like Britain. And for this I am profoundly thankful.

Acknowledgements

I would like to thank Rob Berkeley, Wendy Bottero, Caroline Knowles and Coretta Phillips for their insightful comments on an earlier draft of this piece.

Note

1. Readers will appreciate that this is the correct version of what became a notoriously misquoted passage from the Parekh Report when it was first published. The Report was accused of saying that 'Britishness ... has systematic, largely unspoken racist [the correct wording is "racial"] connotations ...', with all the negative press coverage such a misquoting was bound to generate.

11

Acknowledged Identities: A Common Endeavour or Wider Hostilities?

Kate Gavron

The Young Foundation

In the July 2006 issue of *Prospect* there was an extended cry of despair by an ex-resident of a 1960s estate of social housing on the outskirts of Birmingham. The author, Lynsey Hanley, spent her childhood and youth living on the almost entirely white estate, and describes her feelings of guilt and relief at having escaped to the world beyond the estate, a world of greater aspiration and generosity of spirit. For what stimulated the article was the election in May 2006 of a BNP councillor in the ward containing the estate. To her, white working-class racism is not an understandable reaction to dislocation of communities, relocation to unfamiliar territory, or fear of loss of work. Instead, what she sees is incurious isolation; disillusion; non-voting indifference to an indifferent world; as she puts it: 'It goes something like this: we were put on council estates because we're working class, and if that's what they're going to do to us, we're going to bloody well stay working class.' In her own life story she knows there are other, better, alternatives, and they include having a more welcoming attitude to change, mobility and newcomers.

This article is interesting not just for the passion with which it is written, but also because it represents a hard-headed look at a community (the people who live on the estate, in this case) some of whom seem, at one level, to have been well treated by the welfare state, yet are prepared to vote for a racist party (although only in pitifully small numbers do they vote at all). They have lost out in the meritocratic race (albeit in most cases through their own lack of effort, as she describes it) and suffer from feelings of failure and hopelessness. As she says, 'These are the people who feel loss and shame most intently in the society we have now: loss and shame that are manifest publicly in bitterness, disgust and loathing.'

This article is a useful addition to recent writing that has resulted from national soul-searching following the BNP's (relative) success in the May local elections. Analyses, my own included, have tended to concentrate on the feelings of loss and betrayal experienced by those white working-class communities (and especially families within those communities) who feel they are competing directly, but at a disadvantage, with new migrants and increasing numbers of minority groups for limited state resources. What Hanley reminds us is that there are white working-class areas which share the same xenophobic attitudes without having experienced any direct competition or conflict with members of the groups for which they express hostility. This wider hostility, coupled with the growing distance of these communities from the mainstream political process, is in itself one argument for the importance of the search for successful community cohesion policies.

In this response I concentrate on what the contributors to this book suggest about the design and implementation of successful strategies, by picking up a few points which struck me as I read through their contributions. I also consider various problems emerging from research, of varying levels of complexity.

In terms of what works, firstly, and perhaps obviously, contributors who have knowledge of on-the-ground initiatives emphasize the importance of effective communication with those affected by community cohesion policies. For example, abstract generalizations about the benefits of immigration to the country as a whole may not be persuasive in places where there are local practical problems to do with a shortage of housing and school places. This links to a point several contributors make: that creating projects in which different groups can participate is vital; arguably, one of the damaging effects of some multicultural policy has been the inadvertent fostering of an atmosphere of competition between different groups. We know how solidarity can build up powerfully over local issues – traffic management; planning controls; temporary crises linked to crime or environmental problems – and cohesion can be encouraged, as Hussain writes, by finding a common endeavour to which everybody can contribute and from which all benefit.

Several contributors mention the pivotal role played by local schools. Johnson comments on research that shows increasing racial and religious segregation in schools, and yet schools can be vital places for bonding (Clarke et al., Wetherell). Clarke et al. describe the problems resulting from the closure of schools in the areas where they carried out research; not only did the areas lose common and crucial points of contact for children and parents, but children found themselves scattered to other areas, in some cases to be educated with their 'traditional' rivals. In one of their examples most of the pupils are white; the advantages of school-gate meeting and mixing are even more important where the school population consists of several (or many) ethnic groups, who may have little other social interaction with one another. These findings point strongly towards cherishing local schools as the places above all others where contacts between pupils and parents can grow and be strengthened, and to the desirability of doing everything possible to minimize segregation in school populations. This in turn raises a fundamental question about the desirability and limits of 'parental choice' when it can be used, as my own research in Tower Hamlets has found, to exacerbate the segregation of different ethnic or – more easily – religious groups.

The downside of strong cohesion within a community is what it means for relationships with those outside the particular 'community', as Hewstone et al. remind us particularly powerfully. This is the conflict inherent in attempts to create solidarity; some being included leads to others, inevitably, being excluded. Groups partly define themselves by who they exclude. This is shown in Phillips's description of the solidarity among prisoners against Prison Officers; her case demonstrates how the presence of a common enemy can create cohesion, but this is not necessarily a model we would wish to see followed outside prison and, indeed, clashes between young men and the police show how easily dangerous solidarities (on both sides) can be developed.

The emphasis in this book (see Wetherell, for example) tends to be on the benefits of strengthening bonds *between* groups, but there are other dangers if this goes with reducing bonds within (smaller) groups. Strong ties within groups can be valuable, especially for weaker, smaller and – crucially – poorer groups. Many of the deprived minority ethnic communities in our cities are heavily dependent on mutual support systems, especially for the care of the old and the very young, and any initiatives which jeopardized these kinds of mutual support by, for example, dismantling services designed for particular ethnic groups in favour of more generalized supports, may do harm as well as good. This is an example of what is best for individual groups within localities being at odds with what could foster cohesion for a local community as a whole, and reminds us again of the danger of competition over limited resources.

There are other more difficult obstacles to confront when thinking about cohesion, however. In calling for a reassertion of fundamental values, Johnson says 'we all sign up to the equality of women and to equal rights for people whatever their sexual orientation'. In the Britain he (and I) wish to see that is indeed true, but it is very far from the case now, and there are other serious clashes between conflicting but sincerely and profoundly held values which, as in the case of sexual orientation, are obstacles to cohesion. For example, many groups (and castes and classes, including among white people) feel strongly about the importance of marriage within a fixed category. On the face of it, nothing could be more antipathetic to satisfactory cohesion than a refusal to intermarry, combined sometimes with the social expulsion of those who do. And yet this is just one example of the complexities and difficulties that have to be confronted and accommodated within areas of difference.

In addition to this, Hussain and others remind us of the important point that 'communities' themselves are not monolithic, the 'Muslim community' being a good example of this, but are divided by, amongst other things, age, gender and class. Even the strong solidarity among prisoners is outweighed by racial solidarity, as shown by Phillips, as 'high status' criminals such as armed robbers will defend the 'low status' sexual offender of the same ethnic background. This raises the question of what constitute the possible or desirable limits to cultural and religious autonomy, and how they relate to the parallel desire for cohesion and integration. These are difficult questions to grapple with if we are to try to accommodate myriad value systems within one over-riding picture of what it means to be a British citizen. Solidarity is always contingent on circumstances and contexts, as is identity (see Brah, also Johnson).

Finally, there are more obvious and practical reasons why we feel we have lost the communities of yesterday, with their (sometimes illusory) solidity, immobility and homogeneity. Both Tam and Clarke et al. remind us of the accelerating mobility in residence and employment, as people are growing used to moving around the country and between employers. Many people move silently between home, car and workplace, many of them 'bowling alone', in Putnam's words. Fewer people work close to home or live near their co-workers. There is more choice of activity within the home itself. For many, all these changes are welcome signs of growing prosperity and success. For others, however, their mobility may itself be part of their desperate search for security and respect – from self and others – which used to come from a settled and satisfying job and now seems to be rare, as Richard Sennett has described (Sennett, 1998, 2003).

Whatever its motivation, growing mobility inevitably weakens social ties and represents, as Clarke et al. put it, 'a fundamental change in social relations' between individuals who are living in 'temporary communities'. This is perhaps the greatest challenge of all, and the one least amenable to public policy. In a labour market seen as at least European-wide and, at most, global, it is hard to make freedom to move compatible with the putting down of roots that is the background to the more settled communities of the past.

For me, the contributions to this book seem to signpost two important outcomes to aim for, one macro, one micro. In the first place, we have to succeed in the hard task of building a consensus of what it means to be British, in such a way that all ethnic groups, classes and ages (and both genders) can sign up to it: in itself a formidable task. Secondly, on-the-ground local initiatives must encourage cooperation between citizens and communities, rather than exacerbate competition between them, but without losing all the strength that citizens can draw from people they see as 'like themselves' – pre-eminently their families, friends and neighbours.

12

Reasoned Identities: A Committed Relationship

Bhikhu Parekh
University of Westminster and House of Lords

There are several recurrent themes in this excellent collection of papers. I would like to explore two of them in further detail.

Multiculturalism

Unlike the Canadian, Australian, Indian and other discussions of multiculturalism, the British discourse is marked by a striking paradox. Many people welcome the fact that Britain is a multicultural society and delight in its cultural diversity. Some of them however endorse multiculturalism while others reject it. How is it possible to welcome multicultural society but reject multiculturalism? And how can those who agree on the value of cultural diversity take such diametrically opposite views on multiculturalism? There are several explanations, the most important being the two different ways in which the term 'multiculturalism' is generally defined in Britain and elsewhere.

For some multiculturalism stands for cultural isolationism or ghettoization, based on the relativist view that every cultural community is self-contained and self-authenticating and has a right to live by its norms. Outsiders cannot judge or criticize it and should respect its autonomy. Multiculturalism in this sense clearly undermines any kind of shared life. More importantly, it also militates against the multicultural society itself. The latter arises because different cultures do not passively coexist but interact and influence each other, something that multiculturalism defined in this way disallows. Champions of multicultural society therefore see multiculturalism as their enemy, and wage an open or subdued war against it (see Johnson). We might call this a static, isolationist or relativist view of multiculturalism.

Those who welcome multiculturalism, and see no tension between it and multicultural society, define it very differently. For them it stands for the view that every culture has its limitations and benefits from a dialogue with others. Such a dialogue alerts it to new visions of human life, expands its imagination, enables it to look at itself from the standpoint of others, adds to its self-knowledge, and creates the conditions of human freedom and rationality. The dialogue requires that different cultures should both be respected and brought into a creative interplay. It challenges the hegemony of the dominant culture, exposes its biases and limitations, and helps create a composite culture in which they can see something of themselves and which they can own with pride as their common achievement. Multiculturalism in this sense is open, interactive, dynamic and creative. Its main policy concern is to create conditions and devise programmes such that different cultural communities feel valued and respected, are integrated in appropriate ways, and interact within an agreed system of rights and obligations. It is basically a celebration and philosophical justification of multicultural society (see Clarke, Gilmour and Garner). We might call this an interactive, dialogical or pluralist view of multiculturalism.

The two senses of multiculturalism could not be more different. The first is multi-culturalism, the second multicultural-ism. The former is committed to the plurality of self-contained cultures, the latter to interactive cultural diversity and a single but internally plural composite culture. The first sense of the term is largely limited to some philosophers and to nationalist writers opposed to multicultural society. The second sense is older in its origin and more common. This is how the term is used in Canada, Australia and other countries that pioneered and remain committed to multiculturalism. The British discourse on multiculturalism began in the early 1970s. Although the term was used in both senses, the second dialogical sense was generally dominant, as becomes clear in the Rampton Report, the Swann Report, the Runnymede report on the Future of Multi-Ethnic Britain, and many other academic and popular writings. It is a pity that this discourse has been muddied in recent years by some influential figures, who for their own different reasons have started defining multiculturalism in the first sense of isolation and ghettoization.

In Britain then the term multiculturalism is used in two different senses. Since the participants to the debate fail to distinguish them, they constantly talk past each other. What is more, their internal division gives encouragement and even legitimacy to those opposed to the multicultural society itself. Although we cannot legislate or arrive at a consensus on how the term should be used, we are entitled to expect that those engaged in the debate will take care to ascertain how others use the term, and concentrate on substantive issues rather than engage in a banal verbal warfare.

Identity

The concept of identity is far more complex then is generally appreciated. It was originally used in relation to individuals to answer such questions as how one remains the same in the midst of change, holds together different aspects of one's life in a unitary sense of oneself, and distinguishes oneself from others and defines one's individuality. The tradition of philosophical discourse to which these questions gave rise acquired a new direction and eventually lost much of its coherence when the term identity was appropriated and used to answer different sorts of questions by psychoanalysts, and later by social psychologists and sociologists. It has now entered popular discourse, and has become so inflated that it is in danger of losing its analytical and explanatory power.

Identity basically refers to how one identifies and defines oneself in relation to others. It is a way of announcing to the world and affirming to oneself who one is and how one positions oneself in the relevant area of life (see Clarke, Gilmore and Garner). It is commonly said that an individual has multiple identities, and the which of these one emphasizes depends on the context. This credit-card view of identity, whose echoes one finds in Amartya Sen's otherwise perceptive *Identity and Violence*, is deeply problematic. To say that one 'has' multiple identities is to imply that identities are possessions rather than forms of relationship; also that they are fixed and objective rather than constantly in the making and products of human decisions (see Brah). It also implies that the bearer of multiple identities somehow transcends them all and has a unitary and elusive core. Identities do not and cannot passively coexist either, for they form part of an individual's life and cannot be neatly compartmentalized. They overlap, interact and shape each other (see Rogaly and Taylor).

Identities also conflict and need an ordering principle if their bearer is not to suffer from schizophrenia. Identities are not and cannot be equally important either. The fact that one is tall or dark or a golfer or a Rotarian is not as significant a part of one's life as the fact that one is a mother or a lover. We would worry about the person who said it was. Different identities play different roles in human life, and some of these are more basic. One's sexual identity is a biological fact about oneself, and does not tell one how to lead one's life, including how to define one's sexual identity itself. Ethnic, religious, racial, political, professional and other identities have different logics and modes of operation, and should not be homogenized. Just as no single identity should be essentialized, the idea of identity too should not be essentialized. Since the religious identity is becoming dominant and is supposed to stand in the way of integration, I shall confine my comments to it.

Human beings generally aim to lead more or less coherent lives, and need broad principles and values to guide their choices. The latter constitute their moral identity. Some individuals base these principles on rational grounds and define their moral identity in secular terms. Others embed it in religion. Their religious identity constitutes the axis of their lives and provides the overarching framework within which they define and relate their other identities. Many Christians, Muslims, Jews and others agonize about how they can be good doctors, teachers, husbands and neighbours, asking in each case what their religious values require them to do in these areas. Muslims have gone further, and set up associations of Muslim professionals and even social scientists where they deliberate on how to bring the Islamic perspective to bear on their work.

When individuals privilege their religious identity in this way, difficulties arise. Take British Muslims. Many of them do not just want to be *Muslims in Britain*, treating Britain as a morally neutral territorial space where they happen to live. Rather they take their British citizenship seriously and want to be good Britons. However, they want to be *Muslim Britons* not *British Muslims*, that is, British in a Muslim way rather than Muslims in a British way. The latter privileges their British identity and requires them to read and practise their religion according to British values and practices. They want to do the opposite, and draw on Islam to help them decide the nature and content of their British citizenship (see Dilwar Hussain).

This can take two forms. They might accept British values and practices but derive their grounds and motivations from Islam. Like other Britons they too are loyal to the country and respect its values and institutions, but for their own reasons. This is common in a multicultural society where different cultural communities agree or converge on a common body of values on different meta-ethical grounds.

Being a Muslim Briton can also take another and more intractable form. One might take a stand on one's religious identity, judge British values and practices by it, and accept only those that conform to it. One might, for example, reject the equality or mixing of sexes. This is easily handled, as we have successfully done over the years. A Muslim Briton might go further, privilege the *ummah* over Britain, and conclude that when their demands conflict, the *ummah* should prevail. He might therefore think it perfectly proper, indeed a moral duty, to go and fight against British forces in Afghanistan and Iraq. The logic is impeccable, and it is surprising that many people in Britain were surprised when some young Muslims made that choice. A Muslim Briton who bases his entire life on a particular reading of his religion might also reject the country's secular and 'permissive' ethos and withdraw into an inner world of rage and revolt.

Our biggest challenge is how to respond to this. It would not do to say that all British citizens should privilege their political identity and show undivided loyalty to the country. This is one view, but there are others, and it is not convincing in its absolutist form. The country should certainly matter, but why should it always trump other loyalties? After all, we disobey laws when they violate our conscience or when our government is engaged in an immoral war abroad.

In dealing with someone who wants to be a Muslim Briton, rational discussion is certainly important, and we need to show him why the claims of the *ummah* should be balanced against those of his country and are best pursued in other ways. Such discussion, however, is rarely conclusive and is unlikely to deter him. What is more, his reading of his religion, like that of anyone else, is necessarily shaped by the experiences and assumptions that he brings to it, and cannot be challenged in textual terms alone. We need to ask why he so heavily privileges his religious identity, defines it in such narrow and exclusive terms, and disregards the moral claims of his political identity, and to find ways of altering the way in which he structures and relates these two (and other) identities. The way an individual defines and relates his identities is the result of a complex interplay between his self-understanding and the manner in which he is treated by the wider society. We can do little directly about the former, and should concentrate on the latter.

Individuals become obsessed with a single identity when it is the only one available to them. Since it is their sole source of meaning and pride, their only bond with others, and their only way of forming part of a collective narrative, they tend to define it in sharp and exclusive norms. It is therefore of vital importance that they should acquire other meaningful identities, such as the occupational, the civic, and the political. This requires opportunities to pursue meaningful careers, to participate in local and national affairs, to put down local roots, and so on. All this is rightly stressed in many of the chapters in this collection.

I want to say something about political identity because it is often misunderstood. It is no use exhorting people to become or feel British. Being British must become part of their lived reality, a matter of daily experience, so that it emerges naturally from and is constantly nurtured by their relationships with those around them. It is therefore essential that the wider society should regard all its citizens as its legitimate members, treat them equally with the rest, ensure them equal rights and opportunities, and address the injustices and disadvantages to which some of them might be subject (see Johnson).

We also need to be clear about what we want when we ask people to be British. Being British is one of a range of their identities. It can neither take their place nor dominate them. It should come to terms with them, and within agreed limits respect them. Just as a language can be spoken in different accents, being British must accommodate plurality and allow people to be British in their own different ways. It must also be open and loosely scripted. The religious and ethnic identities, for example, point to fellow-religionists and fellow-ethnics beyond the territorial boundaries of Britain to whom different groups of British citizens might feel attached. There is no reason why such supra-national allegiances should be frowned upon, or detract from their British identity.

Being British basically means three things: commitment to Britain and its people, loyalty to its legal and political institutions, and respect for the values and norms that are central to its way of life. These three are integral to its stability and vitality, and can rightly be demanded of all its citizens. A view of social cohesion that goes beyond this and requires that they intermarry, share a common view of British history, take pride in it, and so on, asks far more than what is possible, necessary and desirable (see Wetherell). Being British is about being committed and bound to Britain, and is a form of relationship. Since the increasingly popular term 'Britishness' is non-relational, and stresses passive attributes, has an essentialist orientation, is inherently vague, and can be easily used to disqualify any group that appears to show insufficient Britishness, it is a source of much confusion and mischief, and is best avoided.

13

Non-binarized Identities of Similarity and Difference

Avtar Brah

Birkbeck College, University of London

The chapters in this collection have amply demonstrated that questions of identity are central to debates about community cohesion. Whether the context is a prison, a segregated neighbourhood in Northern Ireland or a housing estate in Norwich the question of who people think they are, how they define the boundaries around 'us' and 'them' and what follows from their identifications with others proved to be key to understanding both emerging and historical patterns of social relations. Similarly, the policy position statements in Part One of the book demonstrated that the policymaker cannot get very far without bumping up against notions of identity: facts, theories and fantasies of commonality and diversity. In this chapter I want to focus on what we have learnt from the academic debates about identity that may assist the policymaker and the researcher. I want to highlight conceptions of identity I believe we need to take forward into any new dialogues about the best ways of developing shared lives.

The question of difference, diversity and the problematic of identity has been the subject of scholarly contestation for several decades. These categories have been analysed and deconstructed from different disciplinary boundaries but there is no firm consensus about their meaning. And this is so despite the many deconstructionist, poststructuralist, feminist, postcolonial and anti-racist critiques in which the debates have been steeped. The question of identity immediately raises the related one of 'difference'. The challenge, I suggest, is to think about 'difference' in ways in which it becomes the basis of affinity rather than antagonism. The task is to translate academic conceptual debates into discourses that are meaningful within policy arenas so that there can be productive exchange between academic and policy debates. A key question facing us concerns the manner in which we approach the difference of another. It entails undoing the self-referential 'sameness' at the heart of several centuries of 'modernity'. The issue here is one about being able to relate to others without

'Othering' them. In the remainder of this chapter I explore issues about identity and difference that might throw some light on these problems.

Difference and Identity

As noted above, the second half of the 20th century saw the emergence of a plethora of critiques of modernity but the impact of ideas that have been the subject of critique is still widely prevalent. These critiques threw into relief the ways in which European Enlightenment thought came to represent its own particular and subjective outlook as a universal and objective 'world view'. This 'world view' has been challenged in theoretical debate. It has also been questioned by the activities of political movements. For example, struggles against colonialism interrogated western perceptions of the colonized. In asserting their agency the colonized put western ethnocentricism and racism into question. To say this is not to suggest that there is an impervious boundary between the West and the rest of the world, nor that all sections of the 'western' populations subscribe to such views. It is also not the case that western discourses are inhabited solely by 'western' people. On the contrary, once a discourse is established, it begins to have a life of its own, and can be selectively utilized by all manner of groups including those whom it excludes. Similarly, criticisms of claims of European superiority have been mounted not only by non-Europeans but equally vigorously by many Europeans. However, it is nevertheless the case that this discourse underlines western global hegemony. The issue of difference and identity must therefore be addressed in this context.

How to conceptualize 'difference' is a subject that has been discussed by scholars from many different academic disciplines. These subject disciplines range from philosophy and linguistics; through sociology and anthropology; to politics and science. Much has been written from within the purview of analytic frames extant within each subject area. These critiques demonstrate that the concept of 'difference' itself is not pre-given but rather it comprises a constitutive moment in the formation of these academic disciplines (Foucault, 1998). The epistemological drive to differentiate, classify and construct typologies of 'difference', which has formed a major feature of 'modern' episteme, is thus itself a ruse of power. It is often argued that knowledge is power. But this is not invariably so. Rather, power is immanent within *processes* whereby knowledge is *constructed, legitimated, disseminated and deployed.* Power and regimes of knowledge articulate with specific socio-economic, political and cultural institutions and practices, and together they mark specific bodies, subjects, subjectivities and agencies. We are formed as subjects – American, European, South Asian, East Asian, Muslim, Christian, black, white, man, woman, hetero/gay/lesbian/trans/bisexual, and so on – in and through historically specific dynamics of power in particular contexts. The question of European/British identities is intimately tied with discourses and social practices which both constitute and represent us as differently and differentially positioned subjects within and across different modalities of power.

Power, as we know, is immanent within all social, cultural, emotional and psychic processes. The point therefore is not whether a certain 'difference' exists *a priori*. Rather, what is important is the way in which under given historical circumstances an arbitrary signifier – a colour, a body, a religious creed, a social arrangement/custom, or a set of cultural practices – comes to be associated with particular meanings; that is, it becomes 'a certain kind of difference' etched within asymmetrical power relations with specific outcomes and effects.

The use of the word 'difference' as a concept in order to analyse social phenomena is beset with difficulties. This is partly because the words we use as concepts are simultaneously used as part of everyday acts of communication. Thus we tend to assume that we know what commonly used terms such as difference and identity actually mean. This is not wholly incorrect in so far as being a member of a culture is about sharing meanings. But, it is important to bear in mind that, by the time a word becomes part of what Gramsci calls our 'commonsense', it has already been refracted through multiple mediations and is not 'transparently' knowable; certainly, it cannot mean the same thing to everyone in precisely the same way. Moreover, commonsense terminology assumes even more opaqueness when used as theoretical concepts with their esoteric meanings. Finally, there is the problem of reification whereby fluid and continually changing phenomena that we heuristically define as economic, political, cultural, psychological or psychic are objectified into things. A significant implication of this for scholars and policymakers is that we try as far as possible to clearly indicate the precise sense in which a concept is being used.

The need for interrogating the idea and concept of 'difference' remains important for both political and analytical reasons. Politically, it is important that we continually address and challenge practices that subordinate, suppress, oppress or exploit people deemed to be 'unacceptably different'. Constructions and representations of 'difference', which are used to legitimize such practices as racism, sexism, homophobia, class inequity and inequality, rape, torture, massacre, genocide, in the name of politics, are unacceptable. Essentially we need to foster networks of solidarity and connectivity without erasing the uniqueness of others. Equally, we need to recognize the 'difference' of another without falling into simplistic relativism.

The concept of difference cannot be analysed within the confines of a single academic discipline: its very complexity reveals the limits of disciplinary boundaries. But, interdisciplinary study is not without its own difficulties since the concept of 'difference' is associated with varied and sometimes conflicting, meanings within different theoretical frameworks and subject disciplines. Bringing them together into conversation may, however, lead to 'talking at cross-purposes' unless the distinctive meaning of concepts within differing academic or political fields and the use to which they are put in a given 'creolized theoretical complex' are spelt out, appreciated, and understood. In sociology, for example, the concept of 'class *difference*' has particular resonance over and above the intra-disciplinary differences such the Weberian or Marxian usage of the term. In the fields of philosophy and political theory, the concept of difference has served as the site for developing a critique of the nature of modern western thought with the aim, inter-alia, of decentring the concept of identity associated with the notion of a unified, self-referencing, logocentric, universal subject of 'Reason'. Within linguistics and literary theory, the concept has played its part in the critique of structuralism. Poststructuralist *theories of difference* draw upon insights from philosophy and theories of language in re-thinking the very process of signification. In anthropology and the newly emergent field of cultural studies, attention is centred on the problematic of cultural difference. In feminist theory, the concept of difference has been productively utilized in interrogating *differences* within the category 'woman' – differences of class, ethnicity, generation and so on. In psychoanalysis, *difference signals the trauma of separation* – an ongoing process throughout adulthood but one that is set in train when a baby first sees its own and mother's reflection and '(mis)recognizes' 'self' as different from 'm(o)ther'. In postcolonial and anti-racist theory the idea of 'difference' has been theorized as the relationship of 'metropolis' and 'colony' as mutually constitutive elements: that is, they are both relationally altered by colonialism and imperialism. On the other hand, there are essentialist constructions of 'difference'. An example of this would be the discourse of 'race' as a basis for dividing humanity into categories of inherent, immutable 'difference', the effects of which may be witnessed in the multifarious processes of racism. This partial and far from exhaustive list of different academic/ intellectual discourses of 'difference' has a special bearing on the analytical frame for the study of alterity with which I have been trying to work in that it draws upon insights from these various sources. This frame operates with a complex of concepts designed to address questions of subjectivity and identity in their mutually constitutive entanglements with socio-economic, political, and cultural processes, which, in our era, entail encounters with late capitalist social relations.

As noted above, the problematic of 'difference' is also the problematic of 'identity'. Here Derrida's singularly innovative concept of 'difference' is especially helpful with its simultaneous invocation of 'differ' and 'deferral' (Derrida, 1976, 1982). Identity then, is always in process, never an absolutely accomplished fact. But this does not mean that the human subject cannot or indeed does not *feel* that s/he has identity. Analytically, however, the problematic is to tease out or deconstruct what it means when a subject refers to 'having identity'. How is the term 'identity' being used? What role does it play in a given context? For example, does it reference some unconscious processes that go into the construction of subjectivity, or is the term being used with the intention of foregrounding political identity? This distinction is important even though the two modalities of identity are far from being mutually exclusive. In the former case, inner workings of the subconscious and the unconscious are para-mount, and identity connotes latent processes of psychological invest-ments in culturally specific social ways of doing things in particular ways. So, for instance, a woman may have deep investments in conforming to the ideal of 'good woman' or alternatively she may have far more at stake, emotionally, in following feminist ideals, which may clash with certain social norms. Processes involved in the constitution of *subjectivity* are marked by contradictory processes of identification, projection, dis-avowal, desire and ambivalence so that when a person *proclaims* a specific identity, this is a conscious action seeking to make sense of 'self' in rela-tion to the lived 'social' through the relative opaqueness of inner conflicts of psychic life. In this sense, identity is always de-centred and frag-mented. To the extent that any conscious claim to identity is both *socially and psychically contingent*, the coherence and centred quality of self that is invoked is a deferral of difference, as Stuart Hall has so cogently and per-suasively argued for many years (Hall, 1990, 1996). On the other hand, *political identities* are by definition attempts at creating shared, common goals through conscious agency. The two need to be distinguished in analysis even as they are virtually impossible to separate out in life. There is no simple one-to-one relationship between the 'social' and the 'psychic', but the two are nonetheless mutually interconnected. Despite the many critiques of Althusser's work, his conception of how individuals are 'interpellated' or 'hailed into place' as subjects through the irreducible articulation of psychic and historically specific institutional sites remains illuminating (Brah, 2000, 2002).

Fields of Power – Analytic Attributions of Difference/Identity

So, how might we simultaneously hold on to social, cultural and psychic dimensions in our analysis of the problematic of difference/identity? I have tried to do this in part by analysing 'difference' along four intersect-ing axes as follows:

1. *Difference theorized as social relation in the sociological sense, taking on board the systemic and recursive structures, policies, forces and dynamics of power.* This axis foregrounds economic, social and political aspects concern-ing how, for example, class or gender differences are constructed, or how a black and white body is attributed different meanings in a context of unequal

power relations such as that which, as an example, pertained during transatlantic slavery.

2. *Difference, explored in terms of human experience.* Here, following a long-standing feminist debate, the concept of experience is addressed, not in terms of some notion of transparency of 'knowing', but rather along the lines of considering experience as a way of narrating the symbolic representations (both individual and collective) of material life.

3. *Difference understood as subjectivity,* taking on board emotional life and unconscious processes as well as conscious agency. In order to understand these processes, one has to mobilize psychoanalysis as well as Foucault's notion of discourse and micrologies of power.

4. *Difference analysed in terms of its relationship to formations of identity,* distinguishing social/political identities from processes of subjectivity.

This approach (Brah, 1996) relies on insights from different theoretical traditions. This is made necessary by the complexity of the task of understanding intersectionality between and across *multiple fields of power* – class, gender, racism, caste, ethnicity, nationalism, and so on. Identity, as Michael Taussig (1993) emphasizes, is a relationship not a thing. By definition the socio-cultural and emotional/psychological elements are simultaneously interconnected in this relationship. A related issue concerns the multiplicity of processes of 'Otherness' implicated in social contexts – the 'othering', as the saying goes, of different categories such as women, black people, Muslims, Gypsies or Jews.

The idea of 'Other' too is a frequently invoked term in contemporary writing. It is often used as if its meaning is self-evident when in fact it can signify different things in different discourses. As noted above, in psychoanalysis, 'otherness' is inherent in the critical moment when an infant begins to construct her/his own self-image as separate and distinct from another. This moment of self-recognition or 'identity' emerges from a look 'from the place of the other', in this case the Mother. Self and Other are understood as continually enmeshed from then onwards and become the site of love, hate, envy, pleasure, desire, ambivalence and so on. The psychoanalytic meaning of 'other' is distinct from that associated with the term 'Other' in discussions of social phenomena such as capitalism or colonialism. The latter usage primarily denotes analysis of economic political and cultural institutions and practices through which specific subjects were constructed as innately different or inferior. In the discussion of social relations, especially class, the term 'otherness' refers to discourses and practices associated with class differentiations.

Stuart Hall (Hall, 1996) makes an innovative intervention in this debate when he urges the use of the concept of *'articulation'* (things are connected as much by their difference as similarity) by way of bringing discourse analysis into fruitful conversation with psychoanalysis. He makes use of articulation to underscore 'the notion that an effective suturing of the subject to subject-position requires, not only that the subject is "hailed", but that the subject invests in the position' (p. 6).

In a psychological sense, sameness is impossible. We become human through our sense of unique otherness. In a cultural sense, we need to develop non-oppositional notions of 'similarity and difference'. The 'subject' of subjectivity – one that we encounter in art, music, dance, in moments when we laugh, mourn or sleep – may be elusive but not absent when we act in the world as politicians, or economists, or policymakers. Social/political identities are the more powerful because of psychic investments, although this is not always a fully acknowledged dimension of social life.

Identity as Diasporized Time-Space

Subjective Processes amidst Public Discourse

The facet of identity that general 'identity talk' most frequently mobilizes is that of social/political identity. It is evident that in so far as it is a cultural phenomenon, social identity is intrinsic to social interaction. Political identities are constituted in the process of bringing issues into the public arena. In saying this, I do not wish to endorse the public/private binary that feminist scholars (Pateman, 1988; Spelman, 1988) have so convincingly critiqued. I merely wish to indicate that political identities are constructed in the attempt to secure consensus over the aims of a political project. Hence, in large part, formation of political identities belongs to the arena of conscious action.

Confusion in academic and public discourses arises, however, when the idea of *conscious* agency subsumes processes of subjectivity or what is going on in the emotional landscape of the individual or the collectivity. I have come across strong opposition to post-structuralist notions of identity – as de-centred, fragmented and in process – on the grounds that such a conception does not provide a basis for political action. In reality, the idea of 'identity' as fragmented refers predominantly to the processes of subjectivity, and not necessarily to conscious political action, although conscious action is always marked by 'interior' emotional investments, ruptures and contradictions. Jane Flax (Flax, 1990) makes a helpful distinction between a 'sense of coherent self' which all subjects need for purposeful action, and the problematical idea of an essential core, as if a baby is born with it and the core merely flowers in the fullness of time. Unconscious life continually articulates with conscious action, making voluntaristic notions of agency quite problematic.

Conscious agency and unconscious subjective forces are enmeshed in everyday rituals such as those surrounding eating, shopping, watching football or tennis on television, listening to music, attending political meetings or other social activity. These rituals provide the site on which a sense of belonging, a sense of 'identity', may be forged in the process of articulating its difference from other people's way of doing things. I have called this desire to belong a 'homing desire' (Brah, 1996). But the way in which these 'differences' are understood is what shapes the social outcome: whether such differences are experienced simply as unproblematical ways of doing things differently or invested with emotional valuations of hierarchy, exclusion and unacceptability so that they are perceived as a 'threat to one's way of life'. Such ordinary 'ways of being' at once similar and different can thus become politicized so that fluid, mobile and shifting boundaries that in one case merely signal a particular specificity can now congeal into rigid and impervious boundaries of immutable 'difference'.

In terms of our identifications (or contra-identifications, for that matter), we are all diasporized across multiple social and psychic 'borders', and the 'homing desire' is a desire for security and belonging. The political question is: how do we help create socio-economic and political conditions that are conducive to the fostering of caring and empathetic subjectivities?

If the metaphor of space-time is to serve as an analytical tool, it is necessary to specify the conditions under which particular spatialities and temporalities assume shape within and across particular configurations of power. A focus upon the spatiality of global relations today, for example, draws attention to the varied discourses of globalization emanating from a breadth of sources ranging across the high citadels of IMF, World Bank and Corporate capital; through political discourses of 'nation states'; to the voices of environmentalists and other campaigners; and the narratives of displacement by refugees, asylum seekers and labour migrants. These different discourses need to be distinguished. As Doreen Massey (Massey, 1999) argues, some discourses of globalization ignore economic and political forces that treat people as disposable labour, and subject large sections of the world's population to poverty, hunger and disenfranchisement. Faced with the uncertainties unleashed by radical social change, people become relatively more susceptible to being swept along by appeals to political discourses of identity such as 'patriotism'. Few of us are impervious to the emotional undertones of the discourse of 'my people'. It is not surprising, therefore, when appeals to essentialist forms of group-identity lead to situations of conflict all over the world.

As we have seen above, identity is not an already given thing but rather it is a process. It is not something fixed that we carry around with ourselves like a piece of luggage. Rather, it is constituted and changes with changing contexts. It is articulated and expressed through identifications within and across different discourses. To have a sense of being, say, Muslim is therefore different when confronted with non-Muslims than with friends and family. This sense of self will vary depending on whether the non-Muslims are friendly or hostile. In other words, it will vary according to the histories embedded in the encounter, and the meanings those histories have for the individual and the groups concerned. An encounter of Muslim young men with Sikh young men, for example, may produce identifications as Asians in Britain with a shared history of colonialism as well as shared experience of growing up in Britain. On the other hand, there may be echoes of antagonism between the two groups due to memories of the Partition of India gleaned from parents and the historical political conflict between Sikhs and Muslims. As a consequence of this social background there may ether be solidarity among the men or alternatively their interactions may be characterized by tension. Encounters between Muslim men and white young men of a similar class background, on the other hand, would produce a social and psychological landscape that is marked by both shared formations of class-based masculinities as well as differentiation and divisions produced by racism.

The point is that multiple processes are involved in the construction of what we call identities. They are not a priori givens. Identities mobilize both personal biography and group history. A 'suicide bomber' is thus not a given, but is socially produced. Both social and psychological factors coincide in the constitution of such a category of person. The history of social deprivation associated with areas where Muslim communities are settled, stereotypical representations of Muslims in the media, experiences of Islamophobia and personal circumstances all combine to influence political outcomes. They mark the kind of stake or investment one develops in particular social and cultural arrangements.

Identity – A Work in Progress

A second point that emerges from academic debates about identities is that identity is not singular but is, rather, a plural category. It is now common to talk about multiple identities. This is certainly an improvement on previous discourses of identity. But, many times, this discourse loses sight of the point made above about identity being a process. People will admit that identities are plural but reify the concept by using language such as 'we have multiple identities', as if identity is like an object which you can 'have or possess'. At any given moment, we are positioned across multiple processes of identification which shift and configure into a specific pattern in a designated set of circumstances. It is the circumstances – both social and psychological – that make a particular identity salient and motivating and leading to social action. The circumstances give content to identifications.

The discourses and practices of Islamophobia, for instance, give content to identifications. If you are a Muslim, Islamophobia sets you apart, negatively, from non-Muslims. This may lead to heightened preoccupation with the circumstances of being a Muslim globally. The 'Umah' or the 'transnational Muslim community' becomes salient, drawing attention to other Muslim societies and their plight in the global political order. Attention to global sites of conflict such as Iraq, Chechnya, Kashmir and so on increases a sense of grievance on behalf of all Muslims. Identification with these other societies underscores the experience of

Islamophobia. Religion is politicized nationally and transnationally. Political action then depends on the nature of the political groups an individual comes to subscribe to.

The Unruliness of Identity

This leads me to the third point that needs emphasis. This refers to the distinction made above between political identities and the forces of subjectivity that underpin them. The latter recognize the subjective dimensions, including both conscious factors and the play of the Unconscious. Identities are decentred, fragmented and 'in process'. It is sometimes asked that if identity is fragmentary and continuously in process, how can we talk about political identities that are relatively stable. The answer is not straightforward. The unruliness of identity is especially active at the level of subjectivity where the unconscious holds sway. Political identities are marked by subjectivity but they primarily entail conscious action that seeks to mobilize a group around a specific political agenda. Thus, one can proclaim a Muslim political identity and feel that one has things in common with other Muslims. But at the level of subjectivity, one may experience things quite differently from those whose political visions one may share. There is therefore no simple answer as to why one individual opts for becoming a 'suicide bomber' and another does not. There is no simple formula which can be utilized to come up with a clear-cut answer. But this does not mean that we cannot at all account for social outcomes. For this we need to address the confluence of complex social and psychic dimensions in underpinning the emergence of political identities.

Bibliography

Alexander, C. (2000) *The Asian Gang: Ethnicity, Identity, Masculinity.* Oxford: Berg.

Alexander, C. (2004) 'Imagining the Asian Gang: Ethnicity, Masculinity and Youth after "the Riots"', *Critical Social Policy*, 24 (4): 526–49.

Alexander, C. (2005) 'Embodying Violence: "Riots", Dis/Order and the Private Lives of "the Asian Gang"', in C. Alexander and C. Knowles (eds), *Making Race Matter: Bodies, Space and Identity.* Basingstoke: Palgrave.

Alexander, C., Edwards, R. and Temple, B. (2007) 'Contesting Cultural Communities: Language, Ethnicity and Citizenship', *Journal of Ethnic and Migration Studies* (forthcoming).

Allen, C. (2003) *Fair Justice: The Bradford Disturbances, the Sentencing and the Impact.* London: FAIR.

Allport, G. W. (1954) *The Nature of Prejudice.* Reading, MA: Addison-Wesley.

Amin, A. (2002) 'Ethnicity and the Multicultural City: Living with Diversity', *Environment and Planning A*, 34: 959–80.

Anderson, B. (1983) *Imagined Communities.* London: Verso.

Anderson, B. (1991) *Imagined Communities.* London: Verso.

Appiah, K. A. (2005) *The Ethics of Identity.* Woodstock, Oxon: Princeton University Press.

Archer, L. (2001) '"Muslim Brothers, Black Lads, Traditional Asians": British Muslim Young Men's Constructions of Race, Religion and Masculinity', *Feminism & Psychology*, 11 (1): 79–105.

Back, L. (1996) *New Ethnicities and Urban Culture – Racisms and Multiculture in Young Lives.* London: UCL Press.

Barker, M. (1981) *The New Racism.* London: Junction Books.

Bauman, Z. (1996) 'From Pilgrim to Tourist – or a Short History of Identity', in S. Hall and P. Du Gay (eds), *Questions of Cultural Identity.* London: Sage.

Bauman. Z. (2001) *The Individualized Society.* London: Polity Press.

BBC (2006) 'Minister Says BNP Tempting Voters' (16 April). [at: bbc.co.uk]

Berkeley, R. (2005) 'Civil Renewal, Social Capital and Ethnic Diversity'. *Proceedings of the Runnymede Conference on Social Capital, Civil Renewal and Ethnic Diversity.* London: The Runnymede Trust.

Berkeley, R. (2006) 'An Interview with the Power Commission', *Runnymede's Quarterly Bulletin*, No. 346 (March): 2–5.

Blalock, H. M. (1967) 'Percent Non-white and Discrimination in the South', *American Sociological Review*, 22: 677–82.

Blokland, T. (2003) 'Ethnic Complexity: Routes to Discriminatory Repertoires in an Inner-city Neighbourhood', *Ethnic and Racial Studies*, 26: 1–24.

Boal, F. W., Murray, C. R. and Poole, M. A. (1976) 'Belfast: The Urban Encapsulation of a National Conflict', in S. C. Clarke and J. L. Obler (eds), *Urban Ethnic Conflict: A Comparative Perspective*, Comparative Urban Studies Monograph no. 3, pp. 77–131. Chapel Hill, NC: Institute for Research in Social Science, University of North Carolina.

Bornat, J. (1989) 'Oral History as a Social Movement: Reminiscence and Older People', *Oral History,* 17(2).

Bosworth, M. (1999) *Engendering Resistance: Agency and Power in Women's Prisons.* Aldershot: Dartmouth Publishing Company.

Bosworth, M. and Carrabine, E. (2001) 'Reassessing Resistance', *Punishment & Society*, 3 (4): 501–15.

Bourdieu, P. (1977) *Outline of a Theory of Practice.* Cambridge: Cambridge University Press.

Bowling, B. and Phillips, C. (2002) *Racism, Crime and Justice.* Harlow: Pearson Education.

Brah, A. (1996) *Cartographies of Diaspora, Contesting Identities.* London and New York: Routledge.

Brah, A. (2000) 'The Scent of Memory: Strangers, Our Own, and Others', in A. Brah and A. Coombes (eds), *Hybridity and Its Discontents: Politics, Science, Culture.* London and New York: Routledge.

Brah, A. (2002) 'Global Mobilities, Local Predicaments: Globalization and the Critical Imagination', *Feminist Review* (70).

Brewer, M. B. (1993) 'The Role of Distinctiveness in Social Identity and Group Behavior', in M. Hogg and D. Abrams (eds), *Group Motivation: Social Psychological Perspectives*, pp. 1–16. London: Harvester Wheatsheaf.

Brewer, M. B. and Campbell, D. T. (1976) *Ethnocentrism and Intergroup Attitudes: East African Evidence.* New York: Halstead Press.

Brewer, M. B. and Gaertner, S. L. (2001) 'Toward Reduction of Prejudice: Intergroup Contact and Social Categorization', in R. Brown and S. L. Gaertner (eds), *Blackwell Handbook of Social Psychology: Intergroup Processes*, pp. 451–74. Oxford: Blackwell.

Brewer, M. B. and Pierce, K. P. (2005) 'Social Identity Complexity and Outgroup Tolerance', *Personality and Social Psychology Bulletin,* 31: 428–37.

Brighouse, H. and Swift, A. (2006) 'Parents' Rights and the Value of the Family', *Ethics*, 117(1), October.

Brown, G. (2006) 'The Future of Britishness' (keynote speech to the Fabian Future of Britishness conference, 14 January).[at: http://www.fabiansociety.org.uk/ press_office/]

Brown, R. and Hewstone, M. (2005) 'An Integrative Theory of Intergroup Contact', in M. Zanna (ed.), *Advances in Experimental Social Psychology*, Vol. 37, pp. 255–343. San Diego, CA: Academic Press.

Burgat F. (2003) 'Veils and Obscuring Lenses', in J. Esposito and F. Burgat (eds), *Modernizing Islam – Religion in the Public Sphere in the Middle East and Europe.* London: Hurst and Co.

Burgess, S., Wilson, D. and Lupton, R. (2005) 'Parallel Lives? Ethnic Segregation in Schools and Neighbourhoods', *Urban Studies* 42 (7): 1027–56.

Cabinet Office (2005) *Choice and Voice in the Reform of Public Services. Government Response to the PASC Report – Choice, Voice and Public Services.* London: The Stationery Office. [at: http://www.cabinetoffice.gov.uk/newsroom/news_releases/2005/]

Cairns, E. and Darby, J. (1998) 'The Conflict in Northern Ireland: Causes, Consequences, and Controls', *American Psychologist,* 53: 754–60.

Cairns, E. and Mercer, G.W. (1984) 'Social Identity in Northern Ireland', *Human Relations,* 37: 1095–102.

Cantle, T. (2001) *Community Cohesion: A Report of the Independent Review Team.* London: Home Office.

Carroll, L. (1974) *Hacks, Blacks and Cons: Race Relations in a Maximum Security Prison.* London: D. C. Heath.

Cassidy, C. and Trew, K. (1998) 'Identities in Northern Ireland: A Multidimensional Approach', *Journal of Social Issues,* 54: 725–40.

Castells, M. (1997) *The Information Age, Vol 2: The Power of Identity.* Oxford: OUP.

CFMEB – Commission on the Future of Multi-Ethnic Britain (2000) *The Future of Multi-Ethnic Britain: The Parekh Report.* London: Profile Books for the Runnymede Trust.

Cheliotis, L. K. and Liebling, A. (2006) 'Race Matters in British Prisons: Towards a Research Agenda', *British Journal of Criminology,* 46 (2): 286–317.

Chigwada-Bailey, R. (2003) *Black Women's Experiences of Criminal Justice – Race, Gender and Class: A Discourse on Disadvantage.* Winchester: Waterside Press.

Clarke, S. (2002) 'Learning from Experience: Psycho-social Research Methods in the Social Sciences', *Qualitative Research,* 2 (2): 173–94.

Clarke, S. (2003) *Social Theory, Psychoanalysis and Racism.* London: Palgrave.

Clarke, S. and Garner, S. (2005) 'Psychoanalysis, Identity and Asylum', *Psychoanalysis, culture & Society,* 10 (2): 197–206.

Commission for Racial Equality (1998) *Stereotyping and Racism: Findings from Two Attitude Surveys.* London: CRE.

Commission for Racial Equality (2002) *The Voice of Britain.* London: CRE.

Commission for Racial Equality (2003a) *A Formal Investigation by the Commission for Racial Equality into HM Prison Service of England and Wales – Part 1: The Murder of Zahid Mubarek.* London: CRE.

Commission for Racial Equality (2003b) *A Formal Investigation by the Commission for Racial Equality into HM Prison Service of England and Wales – Part 2: Racial Equality in Prisons.* London: CRE.

Councell, R. (2004) *Offender Management Caseload Statistics 2003, England and Wales.* Home Office Statistical Bulletin 15/04. London: Home Office.

Crewe, B. (2005a) 'Codes and Conventions: The Terms and Conditions of Contemporary Inmate Values', in A. Liebling and S. Maruna (eds), *The Effects of Imprisonment.* Cullompton: Willan Publishing.

Crewe, B. (2005b) 'Prisoner Society in the Era of Hard Drugs', *Punishment & Society,* 7 (4): 457–81.

Crisp, R. J. and Hewstone, M. (1999) 'Differential Evaluation of Crossed Category Groups: Patterns, Processes, and Reducing Intergroup Bias', *Group Processes and Intergroup Relations,* 2: 307–33.

Damer, S. (1989) *From Moorepark to 'Wine Alley': The Rise and Fall of a Glasgow Housing Scheme*. Edinburgh: Edinburgh University Press.

DCLG (2006) *Improving Opportunity, Strengthening Society*. 'One year on – A progress report on the Government's strategy for race equality and community cohesion' (July). London: Department for Communities and Local Government.

Deaux, K. (1996) 'Social Identification', in E. T. Higgins and A. W. Kruglanski (eds), *Social Psychology: Handbook of Basic Principles*, pp. 777–98. New York: Guilford.

Delanty, G. (2003) *Community*. London: Routledge.

Derrida, J. (1976) *Of Grammatology*. Baltimore, MD: Johns Hopkins University Press.

Derrida, J. (1982) *Margins of Philosophy* (trans.). Chicago, IL: Chicago University Press.

Diaz-Cotto, J. (1996) *Gender, Ethnicity and the State: Latina and Latino Prison Politics*. Albany, NY: State University of New York Press.

Dorling, D. (2005) 'Why Trevor is Wrong about Race Ghettos', *The Observer*, 25 September, pp. 14–15.

Dworkin, R. (1978) 'Liberalism', in S. Hampshire (ed.), *Public and Private Morality*. Cambridge: Cambridge University Press.

Edgar, K. and Martin, C. (2004) *Perceptions of Race and Conflict: Perspectives of Minority Ethnic Prisoners and of Prison Officers*. RDS On-line Report 11/04. London: Home Office.

Edgar, K., O'Donnell, I. and Martin, C. (2003) *Prison Violence: The Dynamics of Conflict, Fear and Power*. Cullompton: Willan.

Ellis, T., Tedstone, C. and Curry, D. (2004) *Improving Race Relations in Prison: What Works?* RDS On-Line Report 12/04. London: Home Office.

Faulkner, D. (2006) 'Reflections on the Fabian New Year Conference: Who Do We Want to Be? The Future of Britishness', *Runnymede's Quarterly Bulletin*, No. 346 (March): 6.

Fine, B. (2005) 'If Social Capital is the Answer, We Have the Wrong Questions', in *Social Capital, Civil Renewal and Ethnic Diversity: Procedings of a Runnymede Conference*, pp. 75–81. London: the Runnymede Trust.

Flax, J. (1990) *Thinking Fragments: Psychoanalusis, Feminism and Postmodernism in the Contemporary West*. Berkeley: University of California Press.

Forman, T. (2003) 'From pet to threat? Minority concentration, school racial context and white youths' racial attitudes.' Unpublished manuscript, University of Illinois at Chicago.

Forrest, R. and Murie, A. (1991) *Selling the Welfare State*. London: Routledge.

Foucault, M. (1979) *Discipline and Punish: The Birth of the Prison*. Harmondsworth: Penguin.

Foucault, M. (1998) *Michel Foucault: Aesthetics, Method and Epistemology* (J. D. Faubion, trans. Vol. 2). New York: The New Press.

Frosh, S., Phoenix, A. and Pattman, R. (2002) *Young Masculinities*. Basingstoke: Palgrave.

Gaertner, S. and Dovidio, J. (2000) *Reducing Intergroup Bias: The Common Ingroup Identity Model*. Hove: Psychology Press.

Gallagher, A. M. (1995) 'The Approach of Government: Community Relations and Equity', in S. Dunn (ed.), *Facets of the Conflict in Northern Ireland*, pp. 27–43. New York: St. Martin's Press.

Genders, E. and Player, E. (1989) *Race Relations in Prison*. Oxford: OUP.

Giddens, A. (1986) 'Action, Subjectivity and the Constitution of Meaning', *Social Research*, 53.

Gilchrist, A. (2004) *Community Cohesion and Community Development: Bridges or Barricades*. London: Community Development Foundation and the Runnymede Trust.

Gilroy, P. (1987) *There Ain't No Black in the Union Jack*. London: Hutchinson.

Gilroy, P. (2004) *After Empire: Melancholia or Convivial Culture?* London: Routledge.

Goffman, E. (1961) *Asylums: Essays on the Social Situation of Mental Patients and Other Inmates*. New York: Anchor.

Goffman, E. (1975) *Frame Analysis: An Essay on the Organization of Experience*. Harmondsworth: Penguin.

Goodhart, D. (2004) 'Too Diverse?', *Prospect Magazine* [www.prospect-magazine. co.uk] (February).

Gotovos, A. (2003) 'Minority Discourse, Social State and the Imposition of Identity: Side Effects of the Ideology of Multi-culturalism', in *Gypsy Identities in Europe: Policy and Research*. Greece: University of Ioannina.

Granovetter, M. (1973) 'Strength of Weak Ties', *American Journal of Sociology*, 78: 1360–80.

Grapendaal, M. (1990) 'The Inmate Subculture in Dutch Prisons', *British Journal of Criminology*, 30(3): 341–57.

The Guardian (2006) 'Muslims Who Want Sharia Law Should Leave', 27 February.

Gutmann, A. (2003) *Identity in Democracy*. Woodstock, Oxon: Princeton University Press.

Halfacree, K. H. and Boyle, P. J. (1993) 'The Challenge Facing Migration Research: The Case for a Biographical Approach', *Progress in Human Geography*, 17(3).

Hall, S. (1990) 'Cultural Identity and Diaspora', in J. Rutherford (ed.), *Identity: Community ,Culture, Difference*, pp. 222–37. London: Lawrence and Wishart.

Hall, S. (1992) 'New Ethnicities', in J. Donald and A. Rattansi (eds), *Race, Culture and Difference*, pp. 256–8. London: Sage.

Hall, S. (1996) 'Who Needs Identity?', in S. Hall and P. du Gay (eds), *Questions of Cultural Identity*. London: Sage.

Hall, S. (2000) 'The Multicultural Question', in B. Hesse (ed.), *Un/Settled Multiculturalisms*. London: Zed Press.

Hallinan, M. T. and Teixeira, R. A. (1987) 'Students' Interracial Friendships: Individual Characteristics, Structural Effects and Racial Differences', *American Journal of Education*, 95: 563–83.

Hammerton, A. J. and Thomson, A. (2005) *'Ten Pound Poms': Australia's Invisible Migrants*. Manchester: Manchester University Press.

Henderson, M., Cullen, F. and Carroll, L. (2000) 'Race, Rights, and Order in Prison: A National Survey of Wardens on the Racial Integration of Prison Cells', *Prison Journal*, 80(3): 295–308.

Her Majesty's Inspectorate of Prisons (2005) *Parallel Worlds: A Thematic Review of Race Relations in Prisons*. London: HMIP.

Hewstone, M., Cairns, E., Voci, A., Paolini, S., McLernon, F., Crisp, R. and Niens, U. (2005) 'Intergroup Contact in a Divided Society: Challenging Segregation in

Northern Ireland', in D. Abrams, J. M. Marques and M. A. Hogg (eds), *The Social Psychology of Inclusion and* Exclusion, pp. 265–92. Philadelphia, PA: Psychology Press.

Hewstone, M., Hughes, J. and Kenworthy, J. (2006) *Generalised Intergroup Contact Effects on Prejudice: From Cross-community Contact to Reduced Racial Prejudice in Northern Ireland.* Manuscript in preparation.

Hewstone, M., Tausch, N., Voci, A., Kenworthy, J., Hughes, J. and Cairns, E. (in press) 'Why Neighbours Kill: Prior Intergroup Contact and Killing of Ethnic Out-group Neighbours', in V. Esses and R. Vernon (eds), *Why Neighbours Kill.* Oxford: Blackwell (SPSSi series).

Hewstone, M., Turner, R., Kenworthy, J. and Crisp, R. (2006) 'Multiple Social Categorization Integrative Themes and Future Research Priorities', in R. J. Crisp and M. Hewstone (eds), *Multiple Social Categorization: Processes, Models and Applications* (forthcoming), pp. 271–310. Hove, E. Sussex: Psychology Press (Taylor & Francis).

Hill, M. (1997) *The Policy Process in the Modern State.* London: Prentice Hall.

Hoggett, P. (1992) 'A Place for Experience: A Psychoanalytic Perspective on Boundary, Identity, and Culture', *Environment and Planning D: Society and Space,* 10: 345–56.

Hollway, W. and Jefferson, T. (2000) *Doing Qualitative Research Differently: Free Association, Narrative and the Interview Method.* London: Sage.

Home Office (2001) *Community Cohesion: A Report of the Independent Review Team* (chaired by Ted Cantle). London: The Home Office.

Home Office (2003) *Prison Statistics England and Wales 2002.* Cm 5996. London: Home Office.

Home Office (2004) *2003 Home Office Citizenship Survey: People, Families and Communities.* Research Study 289. London: Home Office.

Home Office (2005a) *Improving Opportunity, Strengthening Society: The Government's Strategy to Increase Race Equality and Community Cohesion.* London: Home Office.

Home Office (2005b) *Statistics on Race and the Criminal Justice System – 2004.* London: Home Office.

Home Office (n.d.) *Respect Action Plan* [at: http://www.homeoffice.gov.uk/documents/respect-action-plan]

Hughes, E. C. (1971) *The Sociological Eye: Selected Papers.* Chicago, IL: Aldine Atherton.

Imrie, R. and Raco, M. (2003) 'Community and the Changing Nature of Urban Policy', in R. Imrie and M. Raco (eds), *Urban Renaissance: New Labour, Community and Urban Policy.* Bristol: The Policy Press.

Irwin, J. and Cressey, D. (1962) 'Thieves, Convicts and the Inmate Culture', *Social Problems,* 10(2): 142–55.

Isal, S. (2006) *Equal Respect – ASBOs and Race Equality.* London: the Runnymede Trust.

Jacobs, J. B. (1977) *Stateville: The Penitentiary in Mass Society.* Chicago, IL: The University of Chicago Press.

Jacobs, J. B. (1979) 'Race Relations and the Prisoner Subculture', in N. Morris and M. Tonry (eds). Chicago, IL: The University of Chicago Press.

Jenkins, R. (1996) 'Categorization: Identity, Social Process and Epistemology', *Current Sociology*, 48(3).

Jewkes, Y. (2002) *Captive Audiences: Media, Masculinity and Power in Prisons.* Cullompton: Willan.

Kalra, V. S. (2002) 'Extended View: Riots, Race and Reports: Denham, Cantle, Oldham and Burnley Inquiries', *Sage Race Relations Abstracts* 27(4): 20–30.

Kelly, R. (2006). Speech on Integration and Cohesion (launch of the Commission on Integration and Cohesion, 24 August) [at: http://www.guardian.co.uk/religion/Story/]

Khan, O. (2006a) 'Grounding Community Cohesion in Democratic Values', *Runnymede's Quarterly Bulletin*, no. 346 (June): 5–6.

Khan, O. (2006b) *Why Preferential Policies Can Be Fair – Achieving Equality for Members of Disadvantaged Groups.* Perspectives Paper, September. London: Runnymede Trust.

Kundnani. A. (2002) 'The Death of Multiculturalism', *Institute of Race Relations* [at: www.irr.org.uk/cantle/index.htm] (24/04/02).

Kymlicka, W. (1989) *Liberalism, Community and Culture.* Oxford: Oxford University Press.

Larkman Project Group (1984) *The Larkman Project Group.* Norwich: University of East Anglia.

LeVine, R. A. and Campbell, D. T. (1972) *Ethnocentrism: Theories of Conflict, Ethnic Attitudes, and Group Behavior.* New York: Wiley.

Levitas, R. (1998) *The Inclusive Society? Social Exclusion and New Labour.* Basingstoke: Palgrave/Macmillan.

Local Government Association (2006) *Leading Cohesive Communities: A Guide for Local Authority Leaders and Chief Executives.* London: LGA Publications.

Lucey, H., Melody, J. and Walkerdine, V. (2003) 'Transitions to Womanhood: Developing a Psychosocial Perspective in One Longitudinal Study', *International Journal of Social Research Methodology*, 6(3): 279–84.

McGhee, D. (2003) 'Moving to "Our" Common Ground – A Critical Examination of Community Cohesion Discourse in Twenty-first Century Britain', *Sociological Review*, 51(3): 376–404.

McGhee, D. (2005) *Intolerant Britain? Hate, Citizenship and Difference.* Maidenhead: Open University Press.

McLaren, V. (2005) 'Civil Renewal – A Matter of Trust?' *Proceedings of the Runnymede Conference on Social Capital, Civil Renewal and Ethnic Diversity.* London: The Runnymede Trust.

Macpherson, W. (1999) *The Stephen Lawrence Inquiry: Report of an Inquiry by Sir William Macpherson of Cluny.* London: Stationery Office.

Margalit, A. and Raz, J. (1994) 'National Self-Determination', in J. Raz (ed.), *Ethics in the Public Domain.* Oxford: Oxford University Press.

Massey, D. (1995) 'The Conceptualization of Place', in D. Massey and P. Jess (eds), *Place in the World?* Oxford: OUP.

Massey, D. (1999) 'Imagining Globalization: Power-geometries of Time-space', in A. Brah, M. J. Hickman and M. Mac an Ghail (eds), *Global Futures: Migration, Environment and Globalization.* Basingstoke: Macmillan.

Miliband, D. (2006) 'More Power to the People.' [at: http://society.guardian.co.uk/localgovt/story/]

Morrison, Z. (2003) 'Cultural Justice and Addressing "Social Exclusion": A Case Study of a Single Regeneration Budget Project in Blackbird Leys, Oxford', in R. Imrie and M. Raco (eds), *Urban Renaissance? New Labour, Community and Urban Policy*. Bristol: The Policy Press.

Mosse, D. (1999) 'Responding to Subordination: Identity and Change among South Indian Untouchable Castes', in J. R. Campbell and A. Rew (eds), *Identity and Affect: Experience of Identity in a Globalizing World*. London: Pluto Press.

NACRO (2000) *Race: A Snapshot Survey*. London: National Association for the Care and Resettlement of Offenders.

Nayak, A. (2003) *Race, Place and Globalization: Youth Cultures in a Changing World*. Oxford: Berg.

Neighbourhood Renewal Unit (2005) *New Deal for Communities 2001–2005: An Interim Evaluation*. London: ODPM.

Newton, C. (1994) 'Gender Theory and Prison Sociology: Using Theories of Masculinities to Interpret the Sociology of Prisons for Men', *Howard Journal of Criminal Justice*, 33(3).

Niens, U., Cairns, E. and Hewstone, M. (2003) 'Contact and Conflict in Northern Ireland', in O. Hargie and D. Dickson (eds), *Researching the Troubles: Social Science Perspectives on the Northern Ireland Conflict*, pp. 123–40. Edinburgh: Mainstream Publishing.

The Observer (2004) 'Equality Chief Branded as "Right Wing"', 4 April.

Okamura, J. (1981) 'Situational Ethnicity', *Ethnic and Racial Studies*, 4(4).

Paolini, S., Hewstone, M., Cairns, E. and Voci, A. (2004) 'Effects of Direct and Indirect Cross-group Friendships on Judgments of Catholics and Protestants in Northern Ireland: The Mediating Role of an Anxiety-reduction Mechanism', *Personality and Social Psychology Bulletin*, 30: 770–86.

Parekh, B. (2006) 'Reply to Goodhart', *Prospect no.* 123 (June) [at: http://www.prospect-magazine.co.uk/]

Pateman, C. (1988) *The Sexual Contract*. Cambridge: Polity.

Pettigrew, T. F. (1997) 'Generalized Intergroup Contact Effects on Prejudice', *Personality and Social Psychology Bulletin*, 23: 173–85.

Pettigrew, T. F. and Tropp, L. R. (2006) 'A Meta-analytic Test of Intergroup Contact Theory', *Journal of Personality and Social Psychology*, 90: 751–83.

Phillips, C. (2005) 'Ethnic Inequalities under New Labour: Progress or Entrenchment?', in J. Hills and K. Stewart (eds), *A More Equal Society? New Labour, Poverty, Inequality and Exclusion*. Bristol: Policy Press.

Phillips, C. and Bowling, B. (2002) 'Ethnicity, Racism, Crime and Criminal Justice', in M. Maguire, R. Morgan and R. Reiner (eds), *The Oxford Handbook of Criminology*. Oxford: OUP.

Phillips, T. (2005) 'After 7/7: Sleepwalking Back to Segregation' (22 September). [at: http://www.cre.gov.uk]

Phinney, J. S., Ferguson, D. L. and Tate, J. D. (1997) 'Intergroup Attitudes among Ethnic Minority Adolescents: A Causal Model', *Child Development*, 68: 955–69.

Poole, M. and Doherty, P. (1996) *Ethnic Residential Segregation in Northern Ireland.* Coleraine: University of Ulster.

Postmes, T. and Branscombe, N. R. (2002) 'Influence of Long-term Racial Environmental Composition on Subjective Well-being in African Americans', *Journal of Personality and Social Psychology*, 83: 735–51.

Power, A. (1996) 'Area Based Poverty and Resident Empowerment', *Urban Studies*, 33(9).

Prison Reform Trust (2004) *Forgotten Prisoners – The Plight of Foreign National Prisoners in England and Wales.* London: Prison Reform Trust.

Public Administration Select Committee (House of Commons) (2005) *Choice, Voice and Public Services. Fourth Report of Session 2004–05.* London: The Stationery Office.

Putnam, R. D. (2000) *Bowling Alone: The Collapse and Revival of American Community.* New York: Simon and Schuster.

Putnam, R. D., (ed.) (2002) *Democracies in Flux: The Evolution of Social Capital in Contemporary Society.* Cambridge: Cambridge University Press.

Ramadan, T. (2005) *Citizenship and Belonging: What is Britishness?* London: Ethnos for the Commission for Racial Equality.

Rampton, A. (1981) *West Indian Children in Our Schools.* London: The Stationery Office.

Rawls, J. (1971). *A Theory of Justice.* Cambridge, MA: Harvard University Press.

Reidpath, D. D. (2003) '"Love Thy Neighbour" – It's Good for Your Health: A Study of Racial Homogeneity and Mortality', *Social Science and Medicine*, 57: 253–61.

'Respect' website [access it at: http://www.respect.gov.uk/]

Rew, A. and Campbell, J. R. (1999) 'The Political Economy of Identity and Affect', in J. R. Campbell and A. Rew (eds), *Identity and Affect: Experience of Identity in a Globalizing World.* London: Pluto Press.

Ripstein, A. (1997) 'Context, Continuity, and Fairness', in R. McKim and J. McMahan (eds), *The Morality of Nationalism.* Oxford: Oxford University Press.

Roccas, S. and Brewer, M. B. (2002) 'Social Identity Complexity', *Personality and Social Psychology Review*, 6: 88–106.

Rogaly, B., Coppard, D., Rana, K., Rafique, A., Sengupta, A. and Biswas, J. (2004) 'Seasonal Migration, Employer–Worker Interactions, and Shifting Ethnic Identities in Contemporary West Bengal', in F. Osella and K. Gardner (eds), *Migration, Modernity and Social Transformation in South Asia.* New Delhi/ Thousand Oaks, CA/London: Sage.

Rogaly, B., Fisher, T. and Mayo, E. (1999) *Poverty, Social Exclusion and Micro-Finance in Britain.* Oxford: Oxfam; London: New Economics Foundation.

Rose, N. (1999) *Powers of Freedom.* Cambridge: CUP.

Runnymede (2005) *Social Capital, Civil Renewal and Ethnic Diversity.* London: the Runnymede Trust.

Runnymede (2006) 'Proposal for Pensions Reform: Implications for Black and Minority Ethnic Communities.' London: the Runnymede Trust. [access this at: http://www.runnymedetrust.org]

Rustin, M. (1991) 'Psychoanalysis, Racism and Anti-Racism', in M. Rustin, *The Good Society and the Inner World,* pp. 57–84. London: Verso.

Seabrook, J. (1973) *City Close-up.* London: Penguin.

Sen, A. (2006) *Identity and Violence: The Illusion of Destiny*. London: Allen Lane.

Sennett, R. (1977) *The Fall of Public Man*. Cambridge: Cambridge University Press.

Sennett, R. (1998) *The Corrosion of Character*. New York: W. W. Norton.

Sennett, R. (2003) *Respect: The Formation of Character in a World of Inequality*. London: Allen Lane.

Shotter, J. (1984) Social Accountability and Selfhood. Oxford: Blackwell.

Sibley, D. (1995) *Geographies of Exclusion: Society and Difference in the West*. London: Routledge.

Sim, J. (1994) 'Tougher than the Rest? Men in Prison', in T. Newburn and E. A. Stanko (eds), *Just Boys Doing Business?: Men, Masculinities and Crime*. London: Routledge.

Simpson, L. (2004) 'Racial Segregation: Measures, Evidence and Policy', *Urban Studies*, 41(3): 661–81.

Sixsmith, A. J. (1988) 'The Meaning and Experience of "Home" in Later Life', in R. Perks and A. Thomson (eds), *The Oral History Reader*. Oxford: OUP.

Smith, A. M. (1992) *New Right Discourses on Race and Sexuality*. Cambridge: Cambridge University Press.

Social Exclusion Unit (1998) *Bringing Britain Together: A National Strategy for Neighbourhood Renewal*. London: HMSO.

Social Exclusion Unit (2002) *Reducing Re-Offending by Ex-Prisoners*. London: Social Exclusion Unit.

Solomos, J. (2003) *Race and Racism in Britain*. Basingstoke: Palgrave/Macmillan

Spalek, B. and Wilson, D. (2002) 'Racism and Religious Discrimination in Prison: The Marginalisation of Imams in their Work with Prisoners', in B. Spalek (ed.), *Islam, Crime and Criminal Justice*. Cullompton: Willan Publishing.

Sparks, R., Battoms, T. and Hay, W. (1996) *Prisons and the Problem of Order*. Oxford: Clarendon Press.

Spelman, E. V. (1988) *Inessential Woman: Problems of Exclusion in Feminist Thought*. London: The Women's Press.

Stephan, W. G. and Stephan, C. (1985) 'Intergroup Anxiety', *Journal of Social Issues*, 41: 157–75.

Strathern, M. (1992) *After Nature: English Kinship in the Late Twentieth Century*. Cambridge: CUP.

Swann, Lord (1985) *Education for All*. London: The Stationery Office.

Sykes, G. M. (1958) *The Society of Captives: A Study of a Maximum Security Prison*. Princeton, NJ: Princeton University Press.

Sykes, G. M. and Messinger, S. L. (1960) 'The Inmate Social System', in G. H. Grosser, R. McCleery, L. E. Ohlin, G. M. Sykes and S. L. Messinger (eds), *Theoretical Studies in the Social Organization of the Prison*. New York, NY: Social Science Research Council; London: Allen Lane.

Tam, H. (2005) 'Civil Renewal and Diversity'. *Proceedings of the Runnymede Conference on Social Capital, Civil Renewal and Ethnic Diversity*. London: The Runnymede Trust.

Tausch, N., Hewstone, M. and Cairns, E. (2006) 'Contact, attitudes and identity among young Catholics and Protestants living in mixed and segregated areas of Northern Ireland.' Manuscript in preparation.

Taussig, M. (1993) *Mimes and Alterity: A Particular History of the Senses*. London: Routledge.

Taylor, C. (1994) *Multiculturalism*, edited by A. Gutmann. Princeton, NJ: Princeton University Press.

Taylor, M. C. (1998) 'How White Attitudes Vary with the Racial Composition of Local Populations: Numbers Count', *American Sociological Review*, 63: 512–35.

The Telegraph (2001) 'Blunkett in Furore over "British Test"', 10 December.

Tonnies, F. (1988) *Community and Society (Gemeinschaft und Gesellschaft)*. Somerset, NJ, and London: Transaction Publishers.

Trew, K. (1986) 'Catholic–Protestant Contact in Northern Ireland', in M. Hewstone and R. Brown (eds), *Contact and Conflict in Intergroup Encounters*, pp. 93–106. Oxford: Basil Blackwell.

Varshney, A. (2003) *Ethnic Conflict and Civic Life: Hindus and Muslims in India*. New Haven, CT: Yale University Press.

Vasta, E., (ed.) (2000) *Citizenship, Community and Democracy*. London: Palgrave.

Wacquant, L. (2001) 'Deadly Symbiosis: When Ghetto and Prison Meet and Mesh', in D. Garland (ed.), *Mass Imprisonment: Social Causes and Consequences*. London: Sage Publications.

Wagner, U., Christ, O., Pettigrew, T. F., Stellmacher, J., Wolf, C. (2006) 'Prejudice and Minority Proportion: Contact Instead of Threat Effects', *Social Psychology Quarterly*, 69: 380–90.

Webster, C. (2002) 'Race, Space and Fear: Imagined Geographies of Racism, Crime, Violence and Disorder in Northern England', *Capital & Class*, 80: 95–122.

Wilkinson, R. G. (2005) *The Impact of Inequality: How to Make Sick Societies Healthier*. London: Routledge/Taylor & Francis.

Willis, P. (1977) *Why Working Class Kids Get Working Class Jobs*. Farnborough, Hants: Saxon House.

Wilson, D. (2003) '"Keeping Quiet" or "Going Nuts": Some Emerging Strategies Used by Young Black People in Custody at a Time of Childhood Being Re-Constructed', *Howard Journal of Criminal Justice*, 42(5): 411–25.

Wolch, J. and DeVerteuil, G. (2001) 'New Landscapes of Urban Poverty Management', in J. May and N. Thrift (eds), *Timespace: Geographies of Temporality*. London/New York: Routledge.

Wood, J. and Adler, J. (2001) 'Gang Activity in English Prisons: The Staff Perspective', *Psychology, Crime & Law*, 7: 167–92.

World Bank (n.d.) Social capital web resource. [at: http://web.worldbank.org/]

Wright, S. C., Aron, A., McLaughlin-Volpe, T. and Ropp, S. A. (1997) 'The Extended Contact Effect: Knowledge of Cross-group Friendships and Prejudice', *Journal of Personality and Social Psychology*, 73: 73–90.

Younge, G. (2005) 'Please Stop Fetishising Integration. Equality is What we Really Need', *The Guardian* (19 September).

Zizek, S. (1993) *Tarrying with the Negative*. Durham, NC: Duke University Press.

Index

academic research and debates, 56, 123–4, 136, 144
affirmative action, 111
Albany Prison, 80
Alexander, Claire, x, 3, 5, 8; *author of Chapter 10*
Allport, Gordon, 48, 104
alterity, 139
Althusser, Louis, 140
Amin, A., 79, 81, 84, 118–19
Anderson, Benedict, 89, 91, 121
antisemitism, 36
anti-social behaviour orders (ASBOs), 41, 54
anxiety within groups, 105
articulation, concept of, 141
assimilation, 33, 115, 118–19
Australia, 131
autonomy, cultural and religious, 129

Back, Les, 98, 121
Bangladeshi communities, 100
Barker, Martin, 99
Bauman, Zygmunt, 9, 96
'belonging', feeling of, 65, 73, 101, 108–9, 142–3
Berkeley, Rob, ix–x, 122; *co-editor*
Blair, Tony, 124
Blunkett, David, 4, 38, 115–16, 120
Boal, F. W., 104
Bosworth, M., 84
Bourdieu, Pierre, 11
Bradford, 28
Brah, Avtar, x, 3, 7–9, 11, 42, 45, 123–4; *author of Chapter 13*
Branscombe, N. R., 108
Brewer, M. B., 109–11
Bristol, 88, 91–4, 98–100, 121
British National Party (BNP), 44, 56, 123, 126
Britishness, 2, 5–6, 9, 29–31, 39, 43, 49–50, 89–90, 116, 118, 121, 124, 129, 133–5, 138
Brixton Prison, 76
Brown, Gordon, 30, 50, 116

Bunting, Madeleine, 39
Burgat, F., 89
Burgess, Simon, 28

Cairns, Ed, x; *co-author of Chapter 9*
Cameron, David, 30
Campbell, D. T., 109
Canada, 131
Cantle Report (2001), 3–4, 42–3, 120
Carrabine, E., 84
Castells, M., 62
Cheliotis, L. K., 83
'choice' agenda, 40–1, 53–6
Christmas, celebration of, 90
citizenship, 52, 115–18, 124
Citizenship Survey (2005), 17, 81
civil society, 4
Clarke, Simon, 2, 6–7, 121, 127, 129; *co-author of Chapter 8*
colonialism, 137, 141,
Commission for Equality and Human Rights, 24
Commission for Integration and Cohesion, 4
Commission for Racial Equality (CRE) 2, 5, 24–8, 30, 32, 76–7, 82, 118
common ingroup model of identity, 109–10
'commonsense' terminology, 138
community
   concept of, 61–2, 73, 87–92
   definitions of, 120–2
   factors detrimental to, 96–8
   identification with, 95–6
   and identity, 91–6, 100–1, 136
community cohesion, 1
   aims of, 6, 35
   breakdown of, 87–8
   and citizenship, 52
   coded message in, 24
   concept of, 125
   criticisms of, 8–9
   definitions of, 3–6, 9, 43, 100
   discourse of, 36, 122–3
   and diversity, 117
   downside of, 128